Future

Anterior

Future Anterior
Volume XII, Number 2
Winter 2015

In This Issue iii

In this Issue

Competing Authenticities
Bryony Roberts
The recent exhibition *Competing Utopias* at the Neutra VDL Studio and Residences in Los Angeles challenges evolving conceptions of "authenticity" within historic-preservation discourse. The analysis undertakes a brief history of the term "authenticity" to consider the shift from valuations of original materials to the more recent interest in environmental, contextual, and intangible conditions. Addressing experimental preservation practices, the article discusses projects that deploy copying and superimposition to thwart intended experiences of authenticity. The analysis of *Competing Utopias* reveals how it challenges both nineteenth- and twentieth-century notions of authenticity by constructing a simulacrum of Eastern Bloc domesticity within Richard Neutra's interiors from the 1960s.

***Original und Reproduktion*: Alexander Dorner and the (Re)production of Art Experience**
Rebecca Uchill
Original und Reproduktion was the title of a 1929 exhibition hosted by a small Hanover art society in which original artworks were displayed alongside replicas. Launched amid a lengthy published debate over the ethics of art facsimiles, the exhibition was overseen by curator Alexander Dorner, one of the more prolific contributors to the debate and perhaps its most radical apologist for the value of art reproductions. From the cautionary traditionalism of Dorner's contemporaries Max Sauerlandt and Kurt Karl Eberlein to the more liberal provocations of Erwin Panofsky—and later reverberations in the work of Walter Benjamin—the debate saw repeated elisions of reproduction, restoration, and exhibition, revealing broader period anxieties about defining and protecting the true nature of artistic experience.

Albert Kahn's Five-Year Plant and the Birth of "Uncertain Space"
Adam Lauder and Lee Rodney
Structural parallels between the disposable "five-year plants" developed by Albert Kahn Associates, in response to the multiple exigencies of wartime planning, and the newly uncertain character of the spaces described by the classical information

Future Anterior
Volume XII, Number 2
Winter 2015

theory of Claude Shannon during the same period is an entry point for critiquing the rhetoric of crisis at the center of preservation discourse in contemporary Detroit. The authors read the conflicting implications of these historic spaces as instantiating Henri Lefebvre's theorization of an emergent "contradictory space," while complicating his narrative of its evolution out of the abstract space brought into representation by European exponents of the International Style by foregrounding the hyperrationalism of Kahn's industrial buildings. In uncovering this longer trajectory of what they term "uncertain space," the authors trouble the neoliberal paradigm of emergency management framing current preservation projects in Kahn's native city while highlighting the potential for resistant readings. Uncertain space emerges as the horizon of sustainability frameworks that developed out of an earlier discourse on obsolescence, of which Kahn's collaborations with Ford of the 1910s and 1920s are enduring embodiments.

Focus on the 2014 Fitch Colloquium
In celebration of the fiftieth anniversary of James Marston Fitch's founding of America's first historic preservation program at Columbia University, the 2014 Fitch Colloquium, organized by Jorge Otero-Pailos, convened extraordinary figures whose work has transformed the contemporary practice of preservation, asking them to reflect on a single idea that, in their mind, will shape the next half-century of preservation. This issue includes summaries of a selection of talks followed by interviews with the speakers. *Future Anterior* editors Kate Reggev, Nicholas Kazmierski, and Alexander Ford conducted the interviews to further explore the new and unexpected ways in which preservationists engage with the urgent challenges of our time, from social inequity to climate change, from the digital revolution to the limits of government.

Michèle Pierre-Louis, former prime minister of Haiti, and executive director of the Knowledge and Freedom Foundation, examined the concept of "resourcefulness." She focused on Haiti's heritage preservation, which is paralyzed in the face of the country's increasingly severe challenges: galloping demography, degraded environment, and economic and political quagmires. Paradoxically, this may be the moment when specific experiences in Haiti involving underprivileged populations will give rise to a new understanding of their own environment, of their own capacity to affect their history in the making, and consequently to see themselves as agents in the preservation of their heritage. A sense of resourcefulness can constitute the basis for a thought-provoking dialogue of universal scope about the value of preservation.

Adam Lowe, founder of Factum Arte, discussed his notion of "datareality." Heritage, he argued, can no longer be thought of in terms of unique immutable objects. Digital technology has thrown heritage into a new reality where scanning and printing, dematerialization and rematerialization, blur the boundary between the physical and the virtual, the tangible and the intangible. The digital is no longer linked only to the virtual and now has a physical presence. According to Lowe, we are witnessing the rise of a new "datareality" that is related but not the same as materiality and that will change how we think and practice preservation.

John Ochsendorf, professor of Civil and Environmental Engineering and Architecture at MIT, engaged the expanding notions of "structure" in historic preservation. For Ochsendorf, preservation straddles the "two cultures" of the sciences and the humanities and therefore demands a deep engagement with both the technical and the cultural aspects of the built environment. Engineering requirements can be the greatest threat to as well as the clearest opportunity for sound stewardship of cultural heritage, and a more nuanced approach must be developed within the emerging discipline of preservation engineering. He showed how his own work attempts to accomplish this by grasping recent developments in preservation engineering and identifying challenges for the decades ahead.

Ilaria Cavaggioni, director and coordinator for architecture of the Superintendence for the Architectural and Landscape Heritage of Venice and Lagoon, discussed the idea of "flexibility." She described how historic buildings today are subject to new and faster dynamics of transformation driven by environmental and social forces that cannot be solved adequately by traditional preservation expertise. We need to imagine new principles of flexibility to adapt to this new reality without sacrificing ideals of quality and continuity. She urged preservationists to change our view of historic objects from static things to elements of a broader developmental process.

Tim McClimon, president of the American Express Foundation, spoke about the notion of "community." He argued that, more than money, preservationists of the future will need to gain new and much-needed exposure to community members — hopefully turning them into future donors and ensuring the future of their historic treasures. He argued that strong corporate partnerships will play a larger role as springboards for public engagement, sustainable tourism, and urban revitalization.

Artist Intervention: *Pink on Beige*
Anya Sirota

Anya Sirota's *Pink on Beige* series assembles recent urban interventions predicated on superimposition, including *General Manifold* (2012), *Pop It Up* (2013), and *Interrobang* (2013). Siding with expediency, provisional aesthetics, and low-fi tectonics, the works are experimental scenarios that exploit the perceived dissonance between contemporaneity and obsolescence in order to investigate preservation as playful adaptation and perceptual renewal. Each project is sited in a polemical context—the Detroit Packard Plant rooftop, a defunct tannery in Amilly, France, and the Federal Screw Works Plant in Chelsea, Michigan—and each responds to a set of physical circumstances by means of experiential insertions. Combining objects, people, and experiences, the sequence of temporary constructs suggests that calibrated superimposition can reveal something about the world that we inhabit and help us discover forms of heritage that might otherwise be overlooked.

Anya Sirota is an interdisciplinary designer and educator and the cofounder of Akoaki and the Metropolitan Observatory of Digital Culture and Representation (MODCaR). She earned her Masters of Architecture from Harvard's Graduate School of Design and is currently on faculty at the University of Michigan.

1. Cantilever Chairs; Palast der Republik (East German, n.d.), from *Competing Utopias: An Experimental Installation of Cold War Modern Design from East and West in One Context,* Neutra VDL Studio and Residences. Photograph by David Hartwell.

Bryony Roberts

Competing Authenticities

Competing Utopias, a recent exhibition at the Neutra VDL
Studios and Residences in Los Angeles, is, in the words of
its curators, "a design collision that should never happen."[1]
Previously the home of Austrian modernist Richard Neutra, the
Neutra VDL compound has been a house museum since 1990,
most recently under the directorship of Sarah Lorenzen. Taking
issue with the conventions of the house museum, Lorenzen
has organized interventions by artists Santiago Borja, Xavier
Veilhan, and, full disclosure, by this author in 2013, which
either inserted sculptural objects or produced new environments within the historic modernist site. The most recent
exhibition, however, moves beyond a confrontation between
new and old to offer a more disarming challenge to familiar
notions of authenticity. Instigated by both the Neutra VDL and
the Wende Museum, which collects Cold War artifacts from
Germany, Eastern Europe, and the Soviet Union, the exhibition
involved removing all of the furniture and decorative objects
of the VDL House and replacing them with equivalent objects
from the Eastern Bloc. Since the VDL House was rebuilt after
a fire in 1965–66, its mid-sixties interior offers a strangely
comfortable context for objects from the other side of the Iron
Curtain, from vintage record players and typewriters to Soviet
children's books and Stasi surveillance equipment. The stylistic
harmony between the Wende collection and Neutra's interiors
produces surprising elisions between communist propaganda
and the postwar Californian lifestyle. But most subversive is
the choice to leave off any labels or explanation, so that visitors to the house do not know what is original and what has
been added. The lack of labels is the key curatorial move that
challenges established conventions for maintaining and curat-
ing authenticity.

Alongside other interventions in the summer of 2014,
such as Alex Lehnerer and Savvas Ciriacidis's reconstructed
Kanzlerbungalow in the German Pavilion in Venice and Fujiko
Nakaya's billowing fog in the Glass House, this exhibition
points to an emerging phenomenon of installations and exhibitions that undermine constructions of authenticity in historical
architecture. Through strategies of copying, versioning, and
disguising canonical spaces, these projects challenge carefully
constructed simulations of historical moments. It is important to note, however, that these are not entirely renegade

Future Anterior
Volume XII, Number 2
Winter 2015

operations but rather the sponsored products of cultural institutions. In part, they manifest a growing liberalism and self-critique in the management of historic buildings, but they also, more profoundly, hold a mirror to the shifting definitions of authenticity within historic preservation discourse.

The maintenance of "authenticity" is assumed to be a primary goal of historic preservation, and yet the term has never had a stable meaning within the discourse and is rarely defined. As a result, the word has encapsulated a range of ideological positions over time, connoting almost opposite meanings from the nineteenth century to the present. Analyzing its historical usage reveals a change from emphasis on original materials toward intangible, environmental qualities, and increasingly permissive attitudes toward copies and imitations. As these changes have transformed global regulations, leading to the designation of full reconstructions as UNESCO World Heritage Sites, experimental practices engaged in copying, imitating, and reproducing monuments have revealed the slippages between intangible heritage and fiction.

Although the word *authenticity* has its origins in antiquity and long usage in the English language, it has a short and tumultuous history within preservation discourse. From the beginning, the word *authentic* was associated with authorship, having its origins in the Greek *authentikos,* meaning "original, genuine, principal"; from *authentes,* meaning "author, or one acting on one's own authority"; derived from *autos* the word for "self."[2] As the term evolved into the Latin *authenticus,* and later the French *authentique,* it continued to evoke that which is "original, genuine," with the subtle duality of that which can be traced to an author versus traced to an authority. The English word *authentic* gains significance in the eighteenth and nineteenth centuries in opposition to the copy or imitation, in an era that witnessed the flourishing of both historical imitation and industrial reproduction. A 1790 definition points directly to the threat of the copy, defining "authentic" as "proceeding from its reputed source or author; genuine (Opp. To counterfeit, forged, etc.)."[3] In the nineteenth century, other fields besides architecture grappled with the problem of verifying authenticity and defining the nebulous term,[4] but the word did not actually appear in architectural debates on restoration. One expects John Ruskin to have introduced the term, since his writings in *The Seven Lamps of Architecture* (1849) and *The Stones of Venice* (1851–53) sowed the seeds for our association of original materials with authenticity. But his evocation of authenticity is indirect, valuing that which has lasted since original construction and which bears "the spirit which is given only by the hand and eye of the workman" (interestingly a collective, rather than singular authorship).[5] Much clearer is his dismissal of restoration as imitation, for "direct and simply copying, it is palpably impossible" and "a Lie from beginning to end."[6]

His nemesis, Viollet-le-Duc, not surprisingly, does not use the word, instead positing in his text on "Restoration" (1854) the importance of "integrity," which is the overall appearance of wholeness and cohesiveness in a work. His "integrity" allows him to justify the copy—to insert himself as a new authority on the appearance of a historic building able to embody the spirit of an original author.[7] Their disagreement implied two versions of tracing authenticity to authorship, one valuing the materials from the moment of creation, the other a reincarnation of the creative vision. In a satirical, imagined dialogue from 1893, Italian conservator Camillo Boito points to the shortcomings of both, with the former preserving fragments that can't add up to a whole, and the latter risking deception and destruction to restore the impression of artistic integrity.[8] Boito opts for a compromise, prioritizing original materials but allowing new supports or replacements that visually contrast with the original.[9] This high-contrast approach formed the basis of the international regulations to come.

In compromising between Ruskin and Viollet-Le-Duc's positions, twentieth-century international regulations hedged against the dangers of destruction and deception but offered contradictory positions on authorship and authenticity. With the formation of international bureaucracies to manage preservation, the bombastic rhetoric of the nineteenth century transformed into the legalese of the twentieth, masking logical contradictions behind the semblance of consensus. Still without mentioning "authenticity," the Athens Charter of 1931 echoes Boito's preference for contrast between old and new to ensure the legibility of authorship. The Charter requires that any new materials used must be distinctly "recognizable," but remarkably allows reinforced concrete to be used and "whenever possible [. . .] concealed," thereby allowing a window for deception.[10] The sanctity of original authorship erodes in the postwar era, in the period following the establishment of UNESCO and ICOM and the drafting of "The International Charter for the Conservation and Restoration of Monuments and Sites" (Venice Charter) of 1964. There the word *authenticity* finally, belatedly, arrives, just as its connotation is about to be transformed. The opening paragraph of the charter declares: "The common responsibility to safeguard [historic monuments] for future generations is recognized. It is our duty to hand them on in the full richness of their authenticity."[11] The word only appears once and is not defined, but initially seems to imply to same approach to original authorship as in the Athens Charter. The regulations require "respect for original materials" and that alterations "be distinguishable from the original so that restoration does not falsify the artistic or historic evidence."[12] But the Venice Charter also contains the seed of much larger changes. Immediately following the word *authenticity,* the "Definitions" section boldly redefines the historic monument, declaring: "The concept of an historic monument embraces not only the single architectural work but also the urban or rural setting."[13] The effects of contextualism and environmentalism, both burgeoning when this document was written in 1964, can be seen in this shift from valuing a monument as an object with a single author to considering entire environments. UNESCO established the World Heritage Committee in 1972 and its subsequent "Operational Guidelines for the Implementation of the World Heritage Convention" from 1977 requires proof of authenticity of both materials and setting, and broadens authenticity to include subsequent authors, stating that "authenticity does not limit consideration to original form and structure but includes all subsequent modifications and additions, over the course of time, which in themselves possess artistic or historical values."[14] As multiculturalism, postcolonialism, and identity politics blossomed in the 1970s and '80s, this definition expanded further until the Nara Document on Authenticity of 1994 recognized the importance of intangible heritage and cultural traditions beyond the confines of Western object-based monumentality.[15] As a result of these cultural tremors, UNESCO's most recent Operational Guidelines for the Implementation of the World Heritage Convention from 2013 considers buildings, groups of buildings, sites, and natural landscapes, and allows that proof of authenticity can be expressed through not only "materials and substance" but also "traditions, techniques, and management systems; language, and other forms of intangible heritage; spirit and feeling; and other internal and external factors."[16]

The valuation of a sense of place, as the confluence of environment, context, and intangible qualities, has led to a more permissive approach to the copy. In the past three decades, UNESCO has shown greater tolerance for complete reconstructions, listing sites on the basis of "associative value" with historic events. The committee approved the post-war reconstruction of Warsaw in 1980 based on its associative value with the historic events of World War II,[17] and later the reconstructed, symbolically important Mostar Bridge in Bosnia-Herzogovina, despite concerns about the preponderance of new material and some historical inaccuracies. In the controversial case of the Mostar Bridge, ICOMOS endorsed in 2005 a "special kind of 'overall' authenticity . . . this *reconstruction* of fabric should be seen as being in the background compared with *restoration* of the intangible dimensions of this

2. Ground Floor—Waiting Room, from *Competing Utopias: An Experimental Installation of Cold War Modern Design from East and West in One Context,* Neutra VDL Studio and Residences. Photograph by David Hartwell.

property."[18] These developments occurred alongside the full reconstructions of architectural landmarks such as Mies van der Rohe's Barcelona Pavilion and Le Corbusier's Pavilion Esprit Nouveau, in which the materials and even the site location, in the case of the Pavilion Esprit Nouveau, were entirely new.[19] Although there is great diversity across global, national, and local regulatory bodies, it is important to note that the global discourse on historic preservation now values not just the maintenance of original materials or the legibility of original authorship but even more the protection of a total world, an environment that encapsulates a historical moment.

Into this context of redefining familiar notions of authenticity enter experimental preservation practices. Under this term, coined by Jorge Otero-Pailos, one can consider curatorial, artistic, and architectural projects that approach preservation not primarily as material conservation but rather as situating historical buildings in contemporary cultural discourses.[20] In the effort to reframe existing architecture in contemporary terms, artists, architects, and preservationists have adopted a range of media and material practices beyond the typical purview of preservation practices, with site-specific installations involving sound, smell, light, video, dance, and theater. Over roughly the past decade, the number of interventions in historic monuments has multiplied, making prevalent the approach to existing buildings as open works to be transformed by contemporary authors. Heritage institutions themselves have increasingly sponsored such approaches, and the recent trend among historic house museums is to commission site-specific art installations. The new art programs at Philip Johnson's Glass House, Le Corbusier's Villa Savoye, the Casa Luis Barragan, Greene and Greene's Gamble House, for example, have produced not just insertions of sculptural objects but also immersive environments whose atmospheric and associative conditions take over the experience of the place. Fujiko Nakaya's recent installation "Veil" at the Glass House, for example, wrapped the house in a dense, artificial fog that made it invisible in the landscape and created a sense of opaque enclosure on the interior, inverting the myth of transparency associated with the house. These all-encompassing, immersive installations walk a delicate line between attracting new audiences to historic landmarks and critically thwarting the touristic imageability and expected simulation of a historical time period.

If UNESCO and ICOMOS have endorsed authenticity as the "intangible dimensions" of a place, then such projects hold a mirror to that definition by conjuring total, immersive environments that question the "authentic" experience of a landmark. While some projects create the "wrong" environment through atmospheric effects, others do so by superimposing one presumed authentic experience onto another. For the German Pavilion at the 2014 Venice Biennale, curators Alex Lehnerer and Savvas Ciriacidis produced a full-scale reconstruction of the West German Kanzlerbungalow [Chancellor Bungalow] in Bonn inside the neoclassical German Pavilion in Venice, famously renovated under Nazi rule. The reconstruction, although fastidious, nonetheless defied authenticity with its brand-new materials and its "wrong" location. Here the copy challenged authenticity not through its semblance of originality but rather through its spatial occupation of another presumably authentic site. The result was that the "intangible dimensions" of neither the Kanzlerbungalow or the German Pavilion remained intact. The *Competing Utopias* exhibition at the Neutra VDL Studio and Residences, also on display in the summer of 2014, offered a similar juxtaposition of historical moments through the superimposition of two historical environments, in this case not through architectural collage but rather the subtle manipulation of décor.

Whereas in the German Pavilion the contrast between the existing and new is strikingly clear, in *Competing Utopias,* the difference is barely perceptible. During the exhibition, Neutra's VDL Studio and Residences housed a range of furniture and artifacts from the Wende collection, arranged to appear as if the Eastern Bloc occupants had just stepped out, with children's toys strewn around, clothes draped on the beds, and books lying open. Only those familiar with the site could recognize the changed furniture and the added accessories, since none of

3. Second Floor—Kitchen, from *Competing Utopias: An Experimental Installation of Cold War Modern Design from East and West in One Context,* Neutra VDL Studio and Residences. Photograph by David Hartwell.

the artifacts from the Wende Museum were labeled. The curation created a different narrative mise-en-scène on each floor, with an East German bureaucrat's office on the ground floor, the home of an East German pilot and his family on the second floor, and a surveillance room on the roof. The intentionally cinematic approach, as director Sarah Lorenzen states, "played with the fiction inherent in house museums, period rooms, and historical reenactments. These pieces of set design are designed to look 'authentic' and to feel more real than the rooms did with the Neutra family's own belongings . . . the hope is that viewers will begin to question the perceived reality (or authenticity) of the original narrative of the house."[21] The exhibition satirizes the kind of packaged stories that docents recite at house museums, but it also challenges both nineteenth- and twentieth-century understandings of authenticity. By obscuring the difference between the inserted artifacts and Neutra's designs, as well as differences between artifacts of different Eastern Bloc origins, the exhibition thwarts our ability to trace artifacts back to their sources, either authorial or cultural. In its cinematic construction of narrative worlds, it also drily satirizes reconstructions of "intangible" heritage that try to evoke total environments of daily life. The critical force of the exhibition is to demonstrate how close the intangible understanding of authenticity comes to fiction, and how political our choices are about which worlds we choose to revive and why. Beyond the critique, it also offers us a new experiential condition of overlapping historical environments, or *gesamtkunstwerks,* in which the convergence of historical artifacts, materials, and spaces conjures divergent cultural worlds.

As argued by Thordis Arrenhius in her book *The Fragile Monument,* preservation is often a matter of changing context. Either through the literal displacement of objects into a museum, as with royal artifacts after the French Revolution,[22] or the construction of new frameworks of perception, as with the rise of photographic documentation,[23] preservation isolates existing elements and frames them within contemporary cultural contexts. Each definition of "authenticity" has led to different means of repositioning historic artifacts. If the valuation of original materials led to a narrowing of focus to physical conservation, and the rise of environmental concerns widened the frame to natural contexts, then the current appreciation for intangible heritage has expanded the context to include networks of language, knowledge, tradition, and craft. The act of transforming an existing site into an "authentic" place entails a change of context without any physical displacement, by moving the work into a plane of cultural significance that codifies behaviors, appearance, and material properties. The construction of authenticity, therefore, operates much like the

4. Penthouse—Surveillance Room, from *Competing Utopias: An Experimental Installation of Cold War Modern Design from East and West in One Context,* Neutra VDL Studio and Residences. Photograph by David Hartwell.

appropriation of readymades in the lineage of conceptual art. Just as Marcel Duchamp turned the urinal into artwork through exhibition, so the experimental practices above recognize the limitless potential of treating historical buildings as readymades. Like Duchamp, they demonstrate how the processes of remaking and resituating an object completely transform its meaning. Their duplications, imitations, and displacements of historical architecture not only critically reveal the disconnection between the object and the frame but also the experiential possibilities of occupying multiple authenticities at once.

Biography
Bryony Roberts is the principal of the research and design practice Bryony Roberts Studio, based in Los Angeles and Oslo.

Notes
[1] *Competing Utopias: An Experimental Installation of Cold War Modern Design from East and West in One Context* took place at the Neutra VDL Studio and Residences in Los Angeles from July 13 to September 13, 2014. It was curated by David Hartwell, Bill Ferehawk, Justin Jampol, Sarah Lorenzen, and Patrick Mansfield. "Competing Utopias" press release, July 30, 2014.
[2] "Authentic; authenticate; authenticity," from Eric Partridge, *Origins: An Etymological Dictionary of Modern English* (London: Routledge, 1966), 33.
[3] "Authentic," from *The Shorter Oxford English Dictionary*, vol. 1 (Oxford: Claredon Press, 173), 134.
[4] For anxiety about authenticity in literature, philology, and exegesis see the concerned text by the Reverend E. C. Richardson on the difference between "Authenticity and Genuineness," in the *Journal of the Society of Biblical Literature and Exegesis* 7, no. 1 (June 1887): 84–89.
[5] John Ruskin, "The Lamp of Memory," in *The Seven Lamps of Architecture* (New York: Farrar, Straus and Giroux, 1979), 184.
[6] Ibid., 184–85.
[7] Viollet-le-Duc, "Restoration," in *The Foundations of Architecture: Selections from the Dictionnaire Raisonée,* trans. Kenneth D. Whitehead (New York: George Braziller, Inc., 1990), 195.
[8] Camillo Boito, "Restoration in Architecture: First Dialogue," trans. Cesare Birignani, *Future Anterior* 6, no. 1 (Summer 2009): 73.
[9] Ibid., 71.
[10] "The Athens Charter for the Restoration of Historic Monuments — 1931," ICOMOS, http://www.icomos.org/en/charters-and-texts/179-articles-en-francais/ ressources/charters-and-standards/167-the-athens-charter-for-the-restoration-of -historic-monuments.
[11] "The International Charter for the Conservation and Restoration of Monuments and Sites (Venice Charter)," *APT Bulletin.* 37, no. 4 (2006): 51.
[12] Ibid.
[13] Ibid.
[14] "Operational Guidelines for the Implementation of the World Heritage Convention," UNESCO, July 1977, http://whc.unesco.org/archive/opguide77a.pdf.
[15] Pamela Jerome, "An Introduction to Authenticity in Preservation," *APT Bulletin* 39, no. 2/3 (2009): 4.
[16] "Operational Guidelines for the Implementation of the World Heritage Convention," UNESCO, July 2013, http://whc.unesco.org/en/guidelines/.
[17] Christina Cameron, "From Warsaw to Mostar: The World Heritage Committee and Authenticity," *APT Bulletin* 39, no. 2/3 (2008): 20.
[18] Ibid., 23.
[19] Neil Levine, "Building the Unbuilt: Authenticity and the Archive," *Journal of the Society of Architectural Historians* 67, no. 1 (March 2008): 15.
[20] See Jorge Otero-Pailos, "Creative Agents," *Future Anterior* 3, no. 1 (Summer 2006): iii–vii.
[21] E-mail conversation between Sarah Lorenzen and author, September 11, 2014.
[22] Thordis Arrenhius, *The Fragile Monument: On Conservation and Modernity* (London: Artifice Books, 2012): 38
[23] See the discussion of photography in the work of Viollet-le-Duc and John Ruskin, Arrenhius, *The Fragile Monument,* 54–84.

1. El Lissitzky (1890–1941). *Abstract Cabinet* (1928). Movable wall construction made of wood, steel lamella, rotating glass vitrine, fabric covering, 330 x 427 x 549 cm. Courtesy of Sprengel Museum Hannover.

Rebecca Uchill

Original und Reproduktion: Alexander Dorner and the (Re)production of Art Experience

Curator Alexander Dorner is best known for his gallery reinstallation and redesign at the Provinzialmuseum in Hanover during the Weimar Republic era. His galleries used painting, lighting, and other types of architectural framing to suggest epochal "realities" to gallery viewers — dark lighting in the medieval galleries (reminiscent of their original church contexts), and an immersive surround of contemporary abstraction in El Lissitzky's *Abstract Cabinet* (1927–28, a proto-installation artwork within which other works of modern art were contained).[1] In his writing as in his praxis, Dorner consistently suggested that the aesthetic experience of an artwork was best conveyed by a complete picture, which for him included placement in an illustrative context, rather than through the material aspects of a cultural object alone. Dorner's cultivation of gallery "atmospheres" to surround objects on view was no idle aesthetic choice within a Weimar Republic art world in transition — an art world debating the terms of curatorial stewardship, deliberating over the virtues of restorations, reevaluating technologies of artistic production, and generally revising the legislatures of a new landscape of museums incorporated in the service of a democratic public.[2] Between 1928 and 1930, all of these seemingly disparate concerns coalesced in a public debate about facsimiles of artworks, to which Dorner was a major contributor. Combating claims that restoration was tantamount to forgery, and comparing the resituating of artworks through the process of museum acquisition to the expanded circulation of art through reproductive technologies, Dorner led the polemic to restore, enhance, and even replicate artistic works. By way of such endeavors, Dorner believed that he could most efficaciously distribute aesthetic effect.

Key to the "Facsimile Debate," as it has come to be known by art history, was a 1929 essay published in the Hamburg art journal *Der Kreis* by Max Sauerlandt, director of the Hamburg Museum für Kunst und Gewerbe.[3] Sauerlandt railed against a prospectus sent to him by a Würtemberg-based metal fabricator, offering a range of prices for variously sized reproductions of the famed thirteenth-century stone statue of the *Bamberger Reiter*. The modern art enthusiast emphatically rejected this kind of fabrication as "fake!" ("gefälscht!"), proposing that the deception inherent in the translation from the medium of stone into that of metal would produce in the viewer a "corruption of

Future Anterior
Volume XII, Number 2
Winter 2015

the senses, of taste, and of artistic feeling" ("Verderbnis der Sinne, des Geschmacks, des künstlerischen Gefühls").[4] The objection was more than a protomodernist defense of medium specificity: Sauerlandt called the "absurd" forgery of the horseman a "barbaric mistreatment" of a "defenseless" original work of art.[5]

Sauerlandt's next article in the September issue of *Der Kreis* argued that reproductions also mistreated their audiences. He singled out a recent exhibition in Hanover in which thirty-five original works were "smuggled" in among reproductions of original artworks.[6] Viewers were challenged to differentiate between the originals and the copies in order to win a prize. Such instruction could only usurp viewers' proper appreciation of original works, Sauerlandt surmised. "A life of false feelings — the worst thing there is! — is the inevitable result."[7] Elsewhere in his article, Sauerlandt took a sarcastic tone, scorning the justification of reproductive "deceptions" on the basis of an "all things to all" ("alles alles") "communist" spirit: "We have pearls — you like them too? Here! Take them in handfuls: deceptively similar wax beads!" Sauerlandt continued: "Drawings by Dürer, Grünewald, Rembrandt? Here they are! 'It is only prejudice that precludes the happy owner of such a replica from having the feeling of owning the original itself!'"[8] Sauerlandt's last line sarcastically quoted art historian Wilhelm Pinder, a likely reference to another recent speech that had invoked the same quote. That talk, bearing the provocative title "On the Possibility of Fidelity to the Original in Replicas of the Plastic Arts (Plaster-Cast Museums)" ("Über die Möglichkeit originaltreuer Nachbildungen plastischer Kunstwerke [Gips-Museen]"), was delivered by Carl G. Heise, head of the Museums für Kunst und Kulturgeschichte in Lübeck, and advocated the merits of reproductions.[9]

Sauerlandt's articles in *Der Kreis* were then followed by an essay by Heise himself, bearing the title "Commitment to the Copy?" ("Bekenntnis zur Kopie?"), which defended the use of reproductions. His article very likely seemed defensive to its readers: in it, Heise justified his own curatorial cultivation of a plaster-cast collection, displayed in Lübeck's Katharinenkirche. Heise asked how these could be simultaneously regarded (by unattributed others) as reflective of a "museum of the future" and denounced by others as "an example of a dangerous, shallow form of conserving art."[10] One finds, in both Sauerlandt's allegations and Heise's justifications, an implicit association between the potential for the reproduction of art objects and fears about their diminishing value and care.

The debates continued over a series of articles, authored by a number of art theorists and museum leaders, in the left-wing Hamburg journal. Erwin Panofsky, at that time a profes-

sor in Hamburg, contributed the longest article to the *Kreis* series. Published in full under the title "Original und Faksimilereproduktion" in a special edition under the *Kreis* imprint, Panofsky's text argued that facsimile reproduction could not approximate "original experience" — that is, the experience of standing in front of an original — but could certainly give a better, albeit "qualified" impression of artistic intent than defaulting only to originals *in absentia*.[11] Panofsky acknowledged that taste of the day favored *Echtheitserlebnis* — that is, seeing, experiencing, and maintaining the "unrepeatable organic singularity" of the material artifact — over *Sinnerlebnis*, the experience of sensing what he called the "conceptual form" of art (which, implicit in this argument, is not necessarily beholden to its materials). Although he perceived this inclination as a contemporary cultural tendency, Panofsky himself did not claim this preference.[12] To begin, he argued, not all artists

3. Erwin Panofsky, "Original and Faksimilereproduktion." Title page, special issue, Der Kreis (Spring 1930). Illustrated in RES: Anthropology and Aesthetics 57/58 (Spring/Autumn 2010): 332. Permission to reprint courtesy of Michael Diers.

Der Kreis. Zeitschrift für künstlerische Kultur

Erwin Panofsky

Original und Faksimilereproduktion

Sonderdruck

Kreis-Verlag, Hamburg 1

intended to collaborate with the weathering of nature; and, in direct response to the articles that had preceded his, Panofsky made a qualified defense of the "polychromatic intruders" in Heise's Lübeck display that allowed a "poor student" such as himself to get an impression of an artist's original intent.[13] Finally, Panofsky also argued there were gradations of importance of material significance—for example, that they are more important in applied arts or "arts and crafts," which are "first and foremost formed material," than in fine arts, which are "first and foremost materialized conceptual forms."[14]

Dorner, then a young director of the *Kunstsammlung* at the Provinzialmuseum in Hanover, also contributed to this published discussion, weighing in decisively in favor of reproductions. He was, in fact, a member of the leadership of the very Hanover art society that presented the exhibition of facsimiles so fiercely decried by Sauerlandt.[15] On view from May through June of 1929 at the Kestnergesellschaft, the exhibition *Original und Reproduktion* placed high-quality print reproductions alongside original artworks on paper and challenged the general public and experts alike to identify the

4. Frans van Mieris the Younger (1689–1763). *Bildnis des Willem van Mieris* (circa 1737). Black and white crayon on paper, 262 x 215 mm. Copyright Hamburger Kunsthalle /bpk. Photograph by Christoph Irrgang.

originals. Works on view included original artworks by Paul Cézanne, Käthe Kollwitz, Claude Lorrain, Pierre-Auguste Renoir, Giovanni Battista Tiepolo, and Hans von Marées, on loan from public collections in Bremen, Hamburg, Hanover, Lübeck, as well as private collections.[16] While the Kestnergesellschaft records pertaining to this exhibition were either destroyed or are missing today, the Hamburger Kunsthalle archives offer a small window into the types of work displayed—on paper, in pen, pencil, crayon, chalk, and graphite.[17] Promotional materials for the exhibition led with the polemic: "PRIZE QUESTION: Which are the originals?" ("PREISFRAGE: Welches sind die

5. Anonymous (Dutch), *Südliche Flusslandschaft* (no date). Pen, pencil, and graphite, 252 x 365 mm. Copyright Hamburger Kunsthalle / bpk. Photograph by Christoph Irrgang.

6. Jan Hackaert (1628–1685), *Südliche Flusslandschaft mit Weg an einem Ufer* (circa or after 1658). Ink and pencil on paper, 201 x 257 mm. Copyright Hamburger Kunsthalle / bpk. Photograph by Christoph Irrgang.

7. Jan Hackaert (1628–1685), *Südliche Gebirgslandschaft* (circa or after 1658). Graphite, ink, and pencil, 179 x 241 mm. Copyright Hamburger Kunsthalle / bpk. Photography by Christoph Irrgang.

Originale?"), challenging audience members to compete to identify the original works of art. A newspaper reporting on the competition concluded that "at first no one wanted to make a serious attempt at answering the question because they all thought it seemed impossible" ("Zunächst wollte niemand sich ernstlich an die Beantwortung der Frage machen, weil es jedem unmöglich erschien"), suggesting that the availability of original objects might be of less importance than the purists contended.[18] No one, not even the experts, found it simple to differentiate the originals from the reproductions.

On the occasion of this exhibition, Sauerlandt, Heise, and other art historians contributed to a June 1929 "survey" on the theme, which was published as an insert in the *Hannoverscher Kurier* and titled "Original oder Reproduktion?"—the exhibition title rendered as a question. Indeed, Sauerlandt's response appeared on the front page under the title "Apologia for the Original" ("Verteidigung des Originals") and formed the core of the second facsimile essay that Sauerlandt would later publish in the September 1929 edition of *Der Kreis*.[19] Dorner's article, arguing for "Facsimiles' Right to Life" ("Das Lebensrecht des Faksimiles"), likewise presaged his later contribution to the *Kreis* debates. Appearing in the March 1930 issue, Dorner's article proposed bringing *in absentia* artworks into the contemporary imagination through facsimiles. Dorner did not altogether forsake the value of original artifacts; he maintained

8. Jan van der Heyden (1637–1712),
*Der Brand eines Hauses auf dem
Domplatz von Antwerpen* (no date).
Graphite and pen, 251 x 118 mm.
Copyright Hamburger Kunsthalle /bpk.
Photography by Christoph Irrgang.

that uniqueness and authenticity were important to the display
of relics. Dorner exemplified his argument with the conjuring
object of Frederick the Great's sword, which he wrested from
the debated degrees of "Erlebnis" due to works of art:

> It is understandable that no agreement can be reached in
> debates on the value of facsimile reproduction. For those
> who are more concerned with preserving the integrity of

PREISFRAGE
WELCHES SIND DIE ORIGINALE?

Um festzustellen, wie weit es den Beschauern noch möglich ist, das Original von der Reproduktion zu unterscheiden, veranstalten wir während der 1. Woche unserer Ausstellung

ORIGINAL UND REPRODUKTION

bis einschließlich Sonntag, den 2. Juni, eine Preisfrage: Welches sind die Originale? Die Ausstellung enthält neben den Reproduktionen etwa 40 Originale. Die Preisfrage bezieht sich auf die in der linken unteren Ecke mit Nummern versehenen Kunstwerke. Auf der Rückseite dieser Karte sind die Nummern der Stücke einzutragen, die Sie für die Originale halten. Es sind 20 Preise. Originalgraphiken, Reproduktionen und Bücher ausgesetzt, die unter die besten Lösungen verteilt werden. Bei Gleichwertigkeit erfolgt die Verteilung nach Los.

KESTNER-GESELLSCHAFT E.V.
HANNOVER KÖNIGSTRASSE 8

9. Original und Reproduktion exhibition invitation card (undated). Alexander Dorner papers (BRM 1), file 448, Harvard Art Museums Archives, Busch-Reisinger Museum, Harvard University, Cambridge, Massachusetts. Reference Number: ARCH.0000.738.

art works of the past than they are with adapting those works to the uses of our time, facsimiles will be anathema. As far as they are concerned, the ancient work of art can only be experienced at first hand, with a fingertip sense of the cracks in the surface *[Fingerspitzerlebnis]*. Indeed, for them the arduous pilgrimage to the work of art is part of the artistic experience; they want the old work of art to stand isolated from the stream of contemporary life.

For the others, the ideal artistic experience *[Kunsterlebnis]* is naturally obtained before the original, but at the same time it is essential that the art of the past have the greatest possible effect on the present. Now, since, practically speaking, the overwhelming majority of people cannot frequently come into contact with outstanding works of ancient art, and since, on the other hand, the facsimile— even according to its detractors—is able to convey up to 99 percent of the effect of the original, they are willing to sacrifice that one percent in the interests of the majority, and will advocate the production of facsimiles. They do so with a good conscience, because what distinguishes an ancient work of art from a historical relic — like Frederick the Great's sword—is the fact that the sword loses all its value if it is not the original, that is, if I cannot put my hand on the spot where Frederick the Great put his. But with a work of art, the purely historical experience is quite separable from apprehending the artist's ideas. . . . The ideal facsimile can convey the full content of the original with a minimum of loss.[20]

ORIGINAL ODER REPRODUKTION?

UMFRAGE AUS ANLASS DER AUSSTELLUNG DER KESTNERGESELLSCHAFT

Die technische Vervollkommnung in der Wiedergabe von Kunstwerken, die unsere Zeit erreicht hat, gibt augenblicklich zu einer lebhaften Erörterung über das Für und Wider der originalähnlichen Reproduktion unter den Kunstkennern Anlass. Dass es für eine kleinere Stadt bei beschränkten Mitteln sinnvoller wäre, sich ein Museum guter Wiedergaben anzuschaffen statt weniger Originale von geringerer Qualität, will auf den ersten Blick einleuchten. Ein Max Sauerlandt führt interessante Argumente dagegen ins Feld. Der Leser wird sich aus den hier abgedruckten Antworten auf unsere Umfrage ein Urteil über diese für die öffentliche Kunstpolitik wie für den privaten Kunstkäufer wichtige Gegenwartsfrage bilden können.

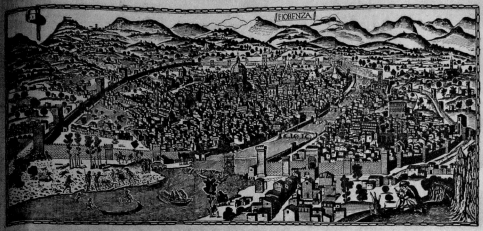

ANSICHT VON FLORENZ

Italienischer Holzschnitt des XV. Jahrhunderts. — Nach der Faksimile-Wiedergabe der Reichsdruckerei.

DR. WILHELM HAUSENSTEIN, MÜNCHEN: EIN MUSEUM AUS WIEDERGABEN

PROF. MAX SAUERLANDT, DIREKTOR DES HAMBURGER MUSEUMS FÜR KUNST UND GEWERBE: VERTEIDIGUNG DES ORIGINALS

Dorner eschewed the *Fingerspitzenerlebnis* of age, the *Kunsterlebnis* of originality, and the overáll *Echtheitserlebnis* of authenticity—all of which posed challenges for a broad public to experience an artwork. Dorner's position in this text drew on an earlier article, from 1926, in which he defended an exhibition of commercial art replicas. Addressed to "he who faces all reproductions of artworks with great skepticism," Dorner established the criterion for exhibiting facsimiles that would be elaborated in the later debate.[21] What was valuable was the "spiritual creation of the artwork as such" ("geistige Schöpfung des Kunstwerks als solche") and not its material and "uniqueness value" ("Einzelheitswert").[22] Dorner's radical populism, and his desire to bring that "spirit" to a wide audience, was elaborated in his *Kreis* submission. Where Panofsky simply observed a popular valuation of *Echtheitserlebnis* that favored materiality over artistic intentionality or viewer reception, Dorner's article expressed total enmity toward that tendency and its implication of limiting popular access to art.

It was only in the valuation of the historical artifact that original materials were crucial. The present-day beholder should be able to project his imagination onto the grip of a sword where a historical figure's hands once rested. At the same time, Dorner believed that the primary obligation of an *artistic* object to its legacy of reception was to grant an experience of artistic form. A facsimile espousing "99 percent" fidelity to original form would thus be a sufficient stand-in for an original art object. To extend Dorner's logic to its furthest extreme, reproduction of a damaged artwork could even be understood as a means for its preservation and not its opposite—contra the Sauerlandt/Heise dialectic that positioned reproduction as tantamount to abandoning the care of artworks.[23] Dorner suggested that invoking approximating the original appearance of an artwork would perpetuate its aesthetic effect, which he considered its essential value. Reproduction was thus cast as a form of preservation through substitution. This was important, Dorner urged, because maintaining the vitality of artistic form was the only way to reincorporate an artwork into the "stream of contemporary life" from which it would otherwise be isolated.

Dorner found both allies with and antagonists to his argument among the other contributors to the *Kreis* debates. Kurt Karl Eberlein, who would soon contribute to the National Socialist culture machine with advocacy for a good "deutsche Kunst" (1933), argued vehemently against photoreproductive copies of art. Eberlein claimed these were "forgeries," and while they may be useful to the master scholar who could use photographic information as a "mnemonic aid," the general public could only be deceived by the artistic losses inherent therein. For Eberlein, it was of paramount importance to retain the purity of original material.[24]

Here Eberlein advanced an argument with Dorner and others on the merits of preserving paintings that had been published in the art dealer's journal *Die Kunstauktion* two years earlier.[25] In that 1928 "Rundfrage" (polled discussion), appearing under the title "Is It Proper to Restore Paintings?" ("Ist es zweckmäßig, Gemälde zu restaurieren?"), Eberlein condemned restorers who filled in lost sections of paint on canvas: "Leave the artistic effect of the 'as-if' to the counterfeiters and dilettantes! Here, we smirk today at everyone who completes an artistic fragment, no matter if it is a work of art, a piece of music, or a poem—only America has such little taste as to organize this kind of competition for commercial reason."[26] To Eberlein, such tastelessness threatened to pervade the field of painting restoration. One can indeed imagine his own smirk while writing: "No educated collector wants the completion of an antique statue, a mosaic ground, or a vase. Yet we still hear again and again of experts raising the incomprehensible argument that paintings are a different case; what is missing in pictures should be replaced!"[27] Eberlein found this preposterous, preferring the idea of a museum of copies to a museum of damaged works that had been subjected to completionist restorations.

Here, Eberlein moved the question of painting restoration directly into one about the production of copies by writing, "Since the loss of art and art theft in our cultured civilization are once again a possibility, and since the European museum will become first and foremost a copy museum, the problem of the scholarly replica—which is only made possible today through museum workshops and the courses they offer—is becoming increasingly urgent. Preserved and lost art complement one another."[28] But in his submission to *Der Kreis,* Eberlein was unwilling to make any kind of concession—not even jokingly—to acknowledging the value of the replica. "As little as one can forge architecture—for it is as singular as an artwork—one can just as hardly forge a painting or drawing as a facsimile reproduction, even if one believes to have the ability to do so a thousand times. A person who wants to forge the form, the body, and the skin of art should not expect us to argue over whether it is permissible to forge artificial skin, artificial patina, artificial antique value. *Forgeries are still forgeries, even if they're not supposed to be forgeries but only to look like them.*"[29] Without citing Alois Riegl directly, in this passage Eberlein used his term *Alterswert* (often translated as "age-value," here as "antique value")—the taste for and value of materials that bear the effects of nature and time.

For Dorner, the notion of the original object placed on exhibition produced its own inherent set of problems, for which the facsimile may be called upon to answer. Because Dorner believed that cultural materials were best valued and canonized by an approximation of their "original" atmosphere, he held that the fundamental recontextualization of every object inserted within a museum was as much a violation against originality as facsimile replica. His *Kreis* article elaborated:

> When an altar is removed from a church, or a painting from a castle, and is placed in an environment that, generated by the interests and needs of the present, is incomprehensible apart from those interests and needs — [that] is a violation of the original purpose of the work of art and the intentions of its creator. A movement calling for the elimination of museums and the return of all works of art to churches and castles would be essentially destructive [and] diminish the use we make of the works of the past, by making them into islands lying isolated in the stream of contemporary life.
>
> A similar case can be made for the facsimile reproduction of old works of art. A medium that evolved organically in response to the needs of our time, facsimile reproduction makes it possible to convey the riches of the art of the past to the greatest number of people. It goes one step further in the direction that was taken by founding museums. But this new step, too, unavoidably violates the original meaning of the works of art. How could it be otherwise, when pieces of an old world are translated into the terms of a new one and put to its uses?[30]

Dorner's galleries reflected his belief that an original historical environment context was fundamental to the appreciation of art — a kind of reparation for what he termed the "violation" wrought by the museum at large. Dorner was not alone in his concern about the ways in which exhibitions deprived artworks of their proper contextual, functional scope. His *Kreis* essay echoes contemporary sentiments, such as those of art theorist Carl Einstein, writing on the renovation of the new Berlin Ethnographic museum four years prior:

> An art object or artifact that lands in a museum is stripped of its existential conditions, deprived of its biological milieu and thus of its proper agency. Entry into the museum confirms the natural death of the work of art, it marks the attainment of a shadowy, very limited, let us call it an aesthetic immortality. An altar panel or a portrait is executed for a specific purpose, for a specific environment; especially without the latter the work is but a dead fragment, ripped from the soil; just as if one had broken a mullion

out of a window or a capital from a column; probably the building had already collapsed. And yet one thing is now isolated: the aesthetic phenomenon—from that very moment the effect of the art object beomes falsified and limited.[31]

Dorner's text resembles Einstein's before it—commenting on the removal of an altarpiece from its original context of encounter and use, and, in the museum, facing the ill fate of being "isolated" from the everyday, as a pure vehicle for aesthetic reception. But where Einstein condemned this process as destructive, Dorner saw it as further justification for the importance of the curator in conveying context, as part of the responsibility for stewardship of art and artifacts on display in a museum.

The matter of separating a cultural object from its traditional milieu—and, in resituating it in the museum, necessarily prioritizing its aesthetic purposes—would be famously tied to anxieties about reproduction in another critical essay written in late 1935 and published in the French edition of the *Zeitschrift für Sozialforschung* in 1936, six years after the last of these articles appeared in *Der Kreis*:

> The uniqueness of a work of art is identical to its embeddedness in the context of tradition. Of course, this tradition itself is thoroughly alive and extremely changeable. An ancient statue of Venus, for instance, existed in a traditional context for the Greeks (who made it an object of worship) that was different from the context in which it existed for medieval clerics (who viewed it as a sinister idol). But what was equally evident to both was its uniqueness—that is, its aura. Originally, the embeddedness of an artwork in the context of tradition found expression in a cult . . . Art history might be seen as the working out of a tension between two polarities within the artwork itself . . . the artwork's cult value and its exhibition value . . . The scope for exhibiting the work of art has increased so enormously with the various methods of technologically reproducing it that, as happened in prehistoric times, a quantitative shift between the two poles of the artwork has led to a qualitative transformation in its nature.[32]

Walter Benjamin's essay "The Work of Art in the Age of Its Technological Reproducibility" similarly distinguished between "traditional" ritual or cult value of a unique art object and the aesthetic values that emerged from its being placed on exhibition. Just as the nature of art's aura shifted as it moved from ritual to exhibition object, so too did technological means of reproduction affect aura in a new way.

A comparable anxiety about the transformation of aura through acts of reproduction or restoration pervaded the Faksimile debates. After refuting "facsimile reproduction" as a form of "forgery," Eberlein's contribution to *Der Kreis* drew to its conclusion with the statement: "Every explanation of why the mysterious, magical, biological 'aura' of a work of art cannot be forged—even though 99 percent of the viewers do not notice the difference—is an offence against the sovereignty of art."[33] Eberlein used the term "aura" (set off in quotes) to represent a fundamental quality of art that would be lost in reproduction, the very questioning of which was a form of disrespect to the category of art overall.[34] Although there is no evidence that Benjamin read the *Kreis* articles on facsimiles (or Eberlein's in particular), it is notable that Benjamin's use of the term "aura" in "The Work of Art" essay was connected to a consideration of art objects and their reproduction. This consti- tuted a departure from his prior uses of the term: in 1930, when he described aura as an ornamental "halo" inherent to all things; or in the following year, when Benjamin suggested that "aura" connoted a "strange web of space and time: the unique appearance of a distance" that—through photography—could operate as a "medium" imbued in and filtering the gaze of a portrait's subject, as well as a quality that realized its "emanci- pation" from object through photography.[35] In "The Work of Art" essay, Benjamin would elaborate the extent of the emancipa- tory project of photography, celebrating that "for the first time in world history, technological reproducibility emancipates the work of art from its subservience to ritual."[36] Eberlein leveraged the term "aura" to argue in favor of retaining the damages to original work, in the name of authenticity. Copies could be made to show the original form of a work but never take its place, because "The problem of art reproductions, of art restoration, is, like everything else, a question of truth and authenticity."[37] From Einstein to Eberlein to Dorner—and, thereafter, to Benjamin—it is clear that the question of the relationship between a work of art and its experience by the beholder within an exhibition context was of primary urgency in these discussions about relocation, restoration, and reproduc- tion of artworks.[38]

Of course, it is no surprise that these debates erupted at the same time that art criticism was attempting to process the widespread use of photography and other devices of mechani- cal reproduction. Dorner's *Hannoverscher Kurier* essay entitled "Das Lebensrecht des Faksimiles" enumerated a series of such apparatuses in its defense of the artistic facsimile: "He who seeks to forbid the making of facsimiles must also ban the movie, the radio, and the gramophone. For these are closely related things."[39] However, Dorner held that no one would undermine a recorded experience of Beethoven's Symphony in C Minor simply because he was not listening "in a crowded concert hall." Indeed, most likely such listening was only accessible with the help of the "good-quality" gramophone reproduction in the first place.[40] Panofsky also seems to have picked up this thread in his own *Kreis* article written the following year:

> A good gramophone record is not "good" because it makes me believe Caruso is singing in the next room, but because it conveys the *musical intention* of his singing precisely. The recording is good because it translates the *largest possible number* of "Caruso-esque" sounds into a sphere of fundamental *differentness,* namely, into the sphere of a *specifically "gramophonic acoustics."* At base, this sphere is determined by an *inorganic-mechanistic character* in even the best recordings: We *hear Caruso's* voice, but *colored* or, if you will, *discolored* by the acoustic determinants of the recording and reproduction equipment, by the axial rotation, the hard rubber, wood, glass, and metal. As such, it now seems to me that a "good reproduction" of a Cézanne watercolor is not "good" because it convinces me of viewing the original. Rather, it is good because it translates the watercoloristic intentions of the artwork to as great an extent as possible into the specific sphere of "reproductive optics." This sphere is also, and should also be, determined by the inorganic-mechanistic character traits: We see the brush strokes and Cézanne's watercolor paper, but colored and, if you will, discolored by the optical determinants of the reproductive machines, the photochemical processes, the *printing* color, and the *printing* paper.[41]

A reproduction bore the marks of its processes, Panofsky acknowledged, and good reproduction should be judged for its ability to convey the most important qualities of the original to the viewer, using the specific optical and technological attributes that were readily understood to be associated with the facsimile. Dorner took this argument much further. He believed that the virtue of the museum was to educate, and he believed that facsimiles could bring the experience of an artwork to the widest audience possible. For Dorner, this was justified because, just as a reproduced or refurbished artwork might not convey the full contour of the original material object, neither could the museum fully encapsulate original tradition, aura, or experience.

In Dorner's prioritization of viewer experience over object stewardship, two wrongs could make a right: for him, the double violations of facsimile production and museum recontextualization could combine to produce the best representation of art's history. Thus, his *Kreis* essay announced: "Since the tendencies of museum and facsimile run parallel to each other, it seems obvious that facsimiles belong in museums that are not able to give a complete overview of the development of art." Although these objects should not be presented as originals or even in the same spaces as original works, they "could substitute for originals in all areas not covered in the museum's collection."[42]

In March 1929, Sauerlandt wrote to Dorner, "With your view on the facsimile I cannot agree. I think the facsimile is just as false and reprehensible as the colorfully painted plaster cast."[43] This is a subject about which Sauerlandt had written another essay that he promised to send soon. It is possible that Sauerlandt was anticipating Erwin Panofsky's forthcoming contribution to *Der Kreis,* which condemned the painted plaster cast for not being a straight mechanical reproduction but involving the "purely personal, even '*artistic*'" human hand. In this case, unlike Panofsky's "gramophonic acoustic," the intervention could not be understood and filtered out by the perceiver; it would provide an additional and detracting layer of affect to the perceptual experience. For Panofsky, "the resulting object is a particular *hybrid, neither a mechanical cast nor an 'artistic' copy,*" a "dubious" object for its removal from the realm of objective mechanical reproduction to that of the "productive optic." Panofsky differentiated between this freehand paint application and the "*inner* freedom of expression that makes a copy cast by Courbet, for example, a true work of art."[44] The distinction between mechanical objectivity and artistic expressivity thus found its hybrid in an artist's copy. Panofsky enabled the conception of a copy as an artistic gesture in a manner that Sauerlandt did not anticipate but Dorner, who had referred to the facsimile as a "medium" unto itself in his *Kreis* article, aspired to cultivate.

It was not until September of that year that the Dorner–Sauerlandt confrontation came to a head. Referring to Dorner's position on the value of facsimiles, Sauerlandt announced that he would not back Dorner's bid to join the Museum Commission. Dorner began a letter-writing campaign, clarifying to Sauerlandt, as well as the two commission members who nominated him, Carl Küthmann and Werner Noack, that he did not believe that museums should collect copies the way they did originals.[45] Perhaps in an attempt to pivot and prove his solidarity in caring about distinguishing original materials from fakes and other post-completion elaborations, Dorner added: "I might also mention that I have discovered a couple of questions about the detection of overpainting on old original paintings, which should at least evince some interest and understanding for the objectives of your association."[46]

Sauerlandt nevertheless succeeded in his efforts to block Dorner. The minutes of the association's meeting on September 23, 1929, in Leipzig show that "after a long debate" ("nach längerer Aussprache") Sauerlandt persuaded Noack and Küthmann to "withdraw their proposal" ("ziehen . . . ihren Vorschlag zurück").[47] Scholar Michael Diers contextualizes this episode as part of a greater effort by Sauerlandt to bar facsimiles from museums altogether. Sauerlandt fought adamantly for this, a threat that "goes to the roots of our existence" ("geht an die Wurzeln unserer Existenz") and twice proposed a Commission resolution against the museum display of facsimiles.[48] Each time—once in October 1929 and once the following year—the proposal was unsuccessful (on the first occasion for reasons of time, the next for lack of sufficient votes).[49]

The debate chronicled here reflected an expansive interest, across the fields of art stewardship, criticism, and theory, in the truth quotient of materials. Debates over truth and falsehood in artworks—and over whether aesthetics were bound to materiality or perceptual reception—continued to unfold in numerous other art publications and exhibitions. Between the years 1928 and 1929, the Berlin journal *Kunst und Künstler* saw multiple pieces by editor Karl Scheffler on the serial topics "Die gefälschte Kunst," naming "truth" as the "fundamental basis of art"; "Echt und Unecht," noting the recent proliferation of articles on the topic in his journal "because nothing is worse than uncertainty"; and "Echt und Falsch," decrying the "embarrassment" of mixed collections of original and reproduced works.[50] A notable exhibition responding to these concerns was hosted by the Folkwang Museum in Essen during the 1930 meeting of the Deutscher Museumsbund at that venue. The Folkwang exhibition also took as its point of departure the theme "Original and Reproduction."[51] Like that at Dorner's Hanover venue, the Essen exhibition presented original works and their reproductions alongside each other.[52] While no museum records of the exhibition remain, Michael Diers assesses that this was primarily intended as a "Korrektur" (correction) to the Kestnergesellschaft exhibition in Hanover.[53] On the occasion of this meeting, Sauerlandt, along with colleagues, received unanimous support for a resolution declaring that "those present consider it their special task to illuminate, through exhibitions and instruction, the essential difference between each reproduction and the original."[54] The resolution included measures whereby museums would use reproductions for didactic purposes and with the requirement to mark these works as reproductions, thus marking a conclusion of sorts to this series of published debates between museum directors over the status of the facsimile.

And yet, the debate over the relationship between the original material of an artwork and its aesthetic efficacies — or how best to convey the "original experience" of an artwork — has continued to pervade the field of art conservation to this decade. In a 2006 essay promoting an expansive definition of authenticity, as provided by the 1994 Nara Document on Authenticity, conservator Pip Laurenson contrasts this with a more "narrow definition" of conservation, focused on its material elements, embraced by a variety of international agencies.[55] A notably consistent element of those latter statements is their common focus on identifying and stabilizing the "original" aspects of a work or elements endemic to its "true nature": this is evident in guidance and ethics statements from the United Kingdom Institute for Conservation of Historic and Artistic Works, the New Zealand Professional Conservators Group, and the International Council of Museums — Conservation Committee, from which Laurenson respectively pulls the following position statements:

> Conservation is the means by which the original and true nature of an object is maintained.
> Conservation is the means by which the true nature of an object is preserved.
> Preservation is action taken to retard or prevent deterioration of or damage to cultural properties by control of their environment and/or treatment of their structure in order to maintain them as nearly as possible in an unchanging state.[56]

Laurenson shows how, as a contested shorthand for "truth" in art, material authenticity has continued to be called upon as a vehicle for a sort of truth in objecthood but not necessarily a means to convey the "truths" of original form or original experience. And art advisor Renée Vara expressly considers the degree of "aura" that remains after a conservation treatment as a metric for appraising contemporary art.[57] The evaluation of "aura" and its association with material austerity continues to pervade discussions about contemporary conservation.

The *Kreis* debates, invoking conflations between the concepts of copies, reproductions, photography, damage, and restorations, showed how period anxieties about material fidelity influenced Weimar Republic art theory and museum policy. At stake were the questions of what should be allowable in the way of enhancing a work of art, as well as its display environs. Contributors took a range of positions: reproductions should stand in for objects that could not be included in the collection, in order to provide populist access; replicas were permissible to help original objects achieve better historical context; reproductions were tantamount to restoration of art objects; replicas were anathema. For Dorner, the true form of art experience was realized only through the visitor, who concertized aesthetics through their subjective reception of replicas, restorations, and original objects alike.

With their allusions to museum education, design, and collection strategies, it is clear that the *Kreis* reproduction debates, and Dorner's contextual contributions to them in particular, were ultimately equally concerned with museum experiences as they were with any epistemic urgencies surrounding photography or plaster casts. Dorner's advocacy for reproductions and for period experiences were connected; the facsimile object may not solve the problem of removing an object from its traditional or historical context (because original objects would always be desired for collections) but the production of a facsimile "atmosphere" might better fuse the object to its originally intended reception. Thus, despite his avant-garde predilections, we see Dorner advocating a version of autonomy that is very different from the modernist myth: Dorner's work of art speaks only from within period atmosphere and context, not in isolation.

Biography
Rebecca Uchill is a Mellon Postdoctoral Fellow at the Center for Art, Science, and Technology and the Department of History, Theory, and Criticism of Art and Architecture at the Massachusetts Institute of Technology.

Notes
[1] According to Dorner's biographer, Samuel Cauman, "The walls and ceilings of the medieval rooms at Hanover were painted in dark colors, for, rooms except for Cistercian examples, medieval churches did not have light interiors or white walls. The rooms receded, permitting only the works of art to stand out and leaving the towering crucifixes and shining altars as the focal points of display. The gold ground and the mystical, soft forms of Late Gothic altarpieces swam in their particular 'reality.'" In *The Living Museum: Experiences of an Art Historian and Museum Director: Alexander Dorner* (New York: New York University Press, 1958), 88.
[2] Dorner introduced the term "atmosphere" in a proposal to describe his renovations to the Rhode Island School of Design Art Museum galleries in the same method as his Hanover galleries. This article uses the term to describe Dorner's work in Hanover as he applied it retrospectively. "Report of the Museum Director on the Activity of the Art Museum: January 1, 1939–April 1, 1939," 3 ff. Alexander Dorner Papers (BRM 1), file 470, Harvard Art Museums Archives, Harvard University, Cambridge, Mass.
[3] See Megan Luke, "The Photographic Reproduction of Space: Wölfflin, Panofsky, Kracauer," *RES: Anthropology and Aesthetics* 57/58 (Spring/Autumn 2010): 339. Also historicized as the "Reproduction Debate"; see György Markus, "Walter Benjamin and the German 'Reproduction Debate,'" in *Moderne begreifen*, ed. Christine Magerski, Robert Savage, and Christiane Weller, 351–64 (Wiesbaden: Deutscher Universitäts-Verlag, 2007).
[4] All translations in this article, unless otherwise noted, are by the author in collaboration with Simon Cowper. Rosanne Altstatt also helped to fine-tune the translations. Thanks is also due to Ines Katenhusen, who read and commented on an early draft of this article.
[5] "Die absurde Fälschung des Bamberger Reiters läßt das Schlimmste befürchten, wenn sich nicht alle Einsichtigen gegen solche barbarische Mißhandlung wehrloser

Kunstwerke zur Wehr setzen." Max Sauerlandt, "Der Bamberger Reiter—gefälscht!" *Der Kreis* 6, no. 3 (1929): 133.

[6] According to Wilfried Basse's review in *Der Kunstwanderer* (August 1929, 560), the actual numbers were thirty-six original artworks out of a total of 104 artworks in the exhibition. As quoted in Luke, "The Photographic Reproduction of Space," 340.

[7] "Ein Leben in falschen Gefühlen—das Schlimmste, was es gibt!—ist die unausbleibliche Folge." Max Sauerlandt, "Original und 'Faksimile-Reproduktion,'" *Der Kreis* 6, no. 9 (1929): 499.

[8] "Wir haben Perlen—Ihr mochtet sie auch? Hier! Nehmt sie aus vollen Händen: täuschend ähnliche Wachsperlen! . . . Zeichnungen von Dürer, von Grünewald, von Rembrandt?—Hier sind sie! Der glückliche Besitzer eines solchen Druckes ist ja 'eigentlich nur noch durch ein Vorurteil von dem Gefühl ausgeschlossen, das Original selbst zu besitzen!'" Ibid., 498.

[9] Heise presented this speech during a 1927 meeting of the museum commission in which Sauerlandt was an active member; the talk was later printed and circulated to all members of the commission on June 15, 1928. Notably, Dorner annotated one copy of this speech and archived it as his own with the label "Vortrag von Dorner" (lecture by Dorner) in his own files, though the proceedings of the twenty-third meeting of the German Museum Association confirm that the lecture and its aforementioned publication was Heise's. "Ueber die Möglichkeit originaltreuer Nachbildungen Plastischer Kunstwerke (Gips-Museen)," Alexander Dorner Papers (BRM 1), file 449.

[10] "[V]on der einen Seite als 'Museum der Zukunft' überschwenglich gefeiert, von der anderen Seite als Musterbeispiel gefährlicher, verflachender Kunstpflege gebrandmarkt worden." Carl Georg Heise, "Bekenntnis zur Kopie?" *Der Kreis* 6, no. 11 (1929): 598–99. Scholar Michael Diers, who was the author of a foundational article about this debate, further suggests that the "educational value" of Heise's cast collection was "endorsed" by his mentor, Aby Warburg. See "Kunst und Reproduktion: Der Hamburger Faksimile-Streit: Zum Wiederabdruck eines unbekannt gebliebenen Panofsky-Aufsatzes von 1930," *Idea* 5 (1986): 135.

[11] "It appears to me that the aesthetic experience of facsimile reproduction and gramophone reproduction does not seek to rival the 'original experience' but is *qualified* in contrast to this experience." Erwin Panofsky, "Original and Facsimile Reproduction," trans. Timothy Grundy, in *Res: Anthropology and Aesthetics 57/58, Spring/Autumn 2010*, ed. Francesco Pellizzi (Cambridge, Mass.: Peabody Museum of Archaeology and Ethnology, 2011), 332. Originally published as "Original und Faksimilereproduktion," *Der Kreis* 7 (Spring 1930).

[12] Ibid.

[13] Panofsky did not wholeheartedly support the use of colored casts, claiming that in "their current, ambiguous state situated between mechanically cast reproductions and freehand copies they are *not yet* facsimile reproductions." But he conceded that, in giving a strong impression of the original vision of the works, they were "still preferable to nothing at all." Panofsky, "Original and Facsimile Reproduction," 334. Panofsky would later elaborate this position—advocating overtly for enabling viewer perception over material austerity—in his 1940 essay "The History of Art as a Humanistic Discipline." In this essay, Panofsky famously offered the suggestion that "it is possible to experience every object, natural or man-made, aesthetically," but, he added, certain objects "demand to be experienced aesthetically because of 'intention.'" Erwin Panofsky, "The History of Art as a Humanistic Discipline," in *Meaning in the Visual Arts: Papers in and on Art History* (Garden City, N.Y.: Doubleday Anchor Books, 1955), 11, 14. Conservator and historian Michael von der Goltz synopsizes the multifold positions on restoration during the Weimar period, including the category of "complementary restoration" that "corresponds to the artist's intention." This latter category, von der Goltz argues, had proponents in "extremely modernist followers." Panofsky would appear to be among these; Dorner's position was even more extreme. Michael von der Goltz, "Restoration Concepts of the 1920s/1930ies [sic] in Germany," in *Theory and History News: Newsletter of the ICOM-CC Working Group 3* 4 (1999): 3.

[14] Panofsky, "Original and Facsimile Reproduction," 335 (see note 11).

[15] While Hanns Krenz was the actual director of the Kestnergesellschaft during the period that the exhibition took place, and thus has been credited as its curator by some sources, Dorner was its most visible public persona and is named as the organizer of the exhibition in others. See Veit Görner et al., *Kestnerchronik* (Hanover: Kestnergesellschaft, 2006), 176; Tobias Wall, *Das unmögliche Museum: Zum Verhältnis von Kunst und Kunstmuseen der Gegenwart* (Bielefeld: Transcript, 2006), 212; Joan Ockman, "The Road Not Taken: Alexander Dorner's Way beyond Art," in *Autonomy and Ideology: Positioning an Avant-Garde in America*, ed. R. E. Somol (New York: Monacelli Press, 1997), 94.

[16] For the list of contributing artists compiled by Joan Ockman, see Ockman, "The Road Not Taken," 95. A partial list of lending institutions is also reproduced in Veit Görner et al., *Kestnerchronik* (Hanover: Kestnergesellschaft, 2006), 101.

[17] Dr. Ute Haug, head of Provenance Research and Historical Archive, Hamburger Kunsthalle, e-mail correspondence with author, June 16, 2014.

[18] "Das Ergebnis der Preisfrage der Kestner-Gesellschaft: 'Welches sind die Originale?'" *Hannover Anzeiger,* June 13, 1929, in Alexander Dorner Papers (BRM 1), file 448.

[19] Heise's "Bekenntnis zur Kopie?" later appeared in *Der Kreis* and was first published in the Hanover newspaper series without the question mark as "Bekenntnis zur Kopie."

[20] Alexander Dorner, "Original and Facsimile," in *Photography in the Modern Era: European Documents and Critical Writings, 1913–1940,* ed. Christopher Phillips, trans. Joel Agee (New York: Metropolitan Museum of Art, 1989), 152. Originally published as "Original und Faksimile," *Der Kreis* 7, no. 3 (1930): 156–58. German original terms inserted by the author.

[21] Alexander Dorner, "Original und Faksimile: Gedanken zur Ausstellung der Piperdrucke in der Kestner Gesellschaft," *2 Beilage zum Hannoverschen Anzeiger* 110, May 12, 1926: 9. The exhibition of prints named in the article's title, and others like it, were also subject to local reviewers' scrutiny over the quality and purpose of the reproductions. See, for example, Broderson, "Die Piper-Drucke," *Hannoverscher Anzeiger* 110, May 12, 1926.

[22] Dorner, "Original und Faksimile: Gedanken zur Ausstellung."

[23] In this respect, Dorner presaged a tendency of our present environment, in which reproductions of failing collection objects may be undertaken as an art conservation imperative. My thanks to conservator Richard McCoy for his consultation on this point.

[24] Kurt Karl Eberlein, "On the Question: Original or Facsimile Reproduction?" translated by Joel Agee in *Photography in the Modern Era: European Documents and Critical Writings, 1913–1940,* ed. Christopher Phillips, 145–50, (New York: Metropolitan Museum of Art, 1989), 148, 147. Originally published as "Zur Frage: 'Original oder Faksimilereproduktion?'" *Der Kreis* 6, no. 11 (1929): 650–52.

[25] For a more extensive treatment of this series of articles, see Michael von der Goltz, "Is It Useful to Restore Paintings? Aspects of a 1928 Discussion on Restoration in Germany and Austria," in *12th Triennial Meeting, Lyon, 29 August–3 September 1999: ICOM Committee for Conservation,* Janet Bridgland, ed. (London: Janes & James, 1999). Von der Goltz points out that restoration was not a common topic of public discussion, least of all by restorers themselves. *Kunstauktion* invited positions on the prompt from artists, restorers, museum directors, and professors. In this debate, Dorner argued for restoration to produce what von der Goltz characterizes as "complementary" "completion" of a painting rather than maintaining visible damages; he, along with Austrian conservator Robert Maurer, resisted the counterarguments that this was tantamount to forgery, instead suggesting that photographic documentation of unrestored work would enhance the educational content and verification process. Von der Goltz, "Is It Useful to Restore Paintings?" 203.

[26] "Die Kunstwirkung des 'als-ob' bleibe den Fälschern und Dilettanten überlassen! Während man schon heute bei uns über jeden lächelt, der ein Kunstfragment fertigmacht, fertigdichtet, fertigkomponiert—nur Amerika hat die Geschmacklosigkeit solcher Preisausschreiben aus Reklamegründen." Eberlein, in response to "Ist es zweckmäßig, Gemälde zu restaurieren? Eine Rundfrage," in *Die Kunstauktion,* June 17, 1928, 8. This translation is an elaboration on one by von der Goltz in "Is It Useful to Restore Paintings?" 204. On the exhibition of cast collections and antique replicas in the United States in the late nineteenth and early twentieth centuries to which Eberlein referred in this quote, and the associated ideologies of American cultural development, see Alan Wallach, "The American Cast Museum: An Episode in the History of the Institutional Definition of Art," in *Exhibiting Contradiction: Essays on the Art Museum in the United States* (Amherst: University of Massachusetts Press, 1998), 38–56.

[27] "Kein gebildeter Sammler [der] die Ergänzung einer antiken Plastik, eines Mosaikfußbodens, einer Vase für das Museum fordert, hört man doch von fachmannischer Seite immer noch oder sogar wieder den unbegreiflichen Einwand, für Bilder wäre das etwas anderes, auf Bildern dürfe man das Fehlende ersetzen!" Eberlein, in response to "Ist es zweckmäßig, Gemälde zu restaurieren?" 8. This translation elaborated from that in von der Goltz, "Is It Useful to Restore Paintings?" 204.

[28] "Da der Kunstverlust und der Kunstraub in unserer kultivierten Zivilisation wieder möglich geworden sind, und da das europäische Museum zunächst auch ein Kopiemuseum sein wird, wird das Problem der wissenschaftlichen Kopie, die erst durch die Museumswerkstätten und ihre Schulung heute möglich ist, immer

drängender. Erhaltene und verlorene Kunst ergänzen sich gegenseitig." Eberlein, "Ist es zweckmäßig, Gemälde zu restaurieren?" 8.

[29] "So wenig man Architektur falschen kann, weil sie ebenso einmalig ist wie das Kunstwerk, ebensowenig kann man ein Bild, ein Blatt durch Faksimileproduktion fälschen, und wenn man es tausendmal zu 'können' glaubt. Wer Kunstkorper, Kunstform, Kunsthaut fälschen will, darf nicht verlangen, daß man mit ihm streite, ob man künstliche Haut, künstliche Patina, künstlichen Alterswert fälschen darf. Fälschungen sind auch dann Fälschungen, wenn sie keine sein sollen, aber wie Fälschungen wirken." Eberlein, "On the Question," 148. This translation elaborated from Joel Agee's (see note 24). Dorner diverged from Eberlein's valuation of *Alterswert*: in a 1921 essay "Über den Sinn der Denkmalpflege" (On the purpose of preserving monuments), published in *Kunstchronik und Kunstmarkt,* Dorner, on the whole a restoration advocate, outlined his position that preservation should be reserved for objects of value, which for him was not defined by age but by significance to historical evolution. Alexander Dorner, "Über den Sinn der Denkmalpflege," in *Kunstchronik und Kunstmarkt,* November 18, 1921, 131–34.

[30] Alexander Dorner, "Original and Facsimile," 152.

[31] Carl Einstein, "Das Berliner Völkerkunde-Museum: Anläßlich der Neuordnung," in *Der Querschnitt,* 6, no. 8 (1926): 588–92. Many thanks to Charles W. Haxthausen, for his direction to this citation and providing me with his English translation, to be published in *Refiguring Vision: The Art Theory and Criticism of Carl Einstein* (Chicago: University of Chicago Press, forthcoming).

[32] Walter Benjamin, "The Work of Art in the Age of Its Technological Reproducibility," in *The Work of Art in the Age of Its Technological Reproducibility and Other Writings on Media,* trans. Edmund Jephcott et al., ed. Michael W. Jennings, Brigid Doherty, and Thomas Y. Levin (Cambridge, Mass.: Harvard University Press, 2008), 24–25. Originally published in an edited French version as "L'oeuvre d'art à l'époque de sa reproduction mécanisée," in *Zeitschrift für Sozialforschung* 5, no. 1 (1936). See Peggy Phalen, "Violence and Rupture: misfires of the ephemeral," in Peggy Phalen, ed. *Live Art in LA: Performance in Southern California, 1970–1983* (New York: Routledge, 2012), 35, note 22. This selection and translation is made from the second version of Benjamin's essay, written in German, from which the first published version drew; these quotations were included in the published version.

[33] Eberlein, "On the Question," 148.

[34] It is not clear whether the quotation marks refer to a prior text or are for emphasis here. My thanks to Prof. Dr. Michael Diers for his assistance in my consideration of this question.

[35] Walter Benjamin, "Hashish, Beginning of March 1930" and "Little History of Photography," respectively. "Hashish, Beginning of March 1930," in *On Hashish,* ed. Howard Eiland (Cambridge, Mass.: Harvard University Press, 2006) 58; "Little History of Photography," in *The Work of Art in the Age of Its Technological Reproducibility and Other Writings,* quoted text from 285, 282, 285. In this analysis I draw from the concise history of Benjamin's use of the term "aura" presented in Charles W. Haxthausen, "'Abstract with Memories': Klee's 'Auratic' Pictures," in *Paul Klee: Philosophical Vision—From Nature to Art,* ed. John Sallis (Chestnut Hill, Mass.: McMullen Museum of Art, Boston College, 2012), 67; I also am indebted to the meticulous tracking of the term in Miriam Bratu Hansen, "Benjamin's Aura," *Critical Inquiry* 32 (Winter 2007), 339, 342. In addition to Haxthausen, other contemporary scholars have noted the correspondences between Benjamin's essay and the *Kreis* articles. György Markus suggests the likelihood that Benjamin saw this series of essays on the basis of his "The Work of Art" essay, taking as a primary concern, as these essays did, the photograph as a means for reproducing other artworks (a rupture from the treatment of photography in Benjamin's "Little History" that preceded it). "It cannot . . . be convincingly proven that he knew about it, though if not, this certainly would be a rather strange case of coincidence." Markus, "Walter Benjamin and the German 'Reproduction Debate,'" 352–53. Megan Luke's essay in *RES* connects Panofsky's claim that photography can be "an entirely personal recreation" with a 1933 essay by Benjamin, who asserted that architectural drawings are a means of production, not strictly reproduction: "Such architecture is not primarily 'seen' but rather is imagined as an objective entity and is sensed by those who approach or even enter it as a surrounding space sui generis, that is, without the distancing effect of the edge of the image space." Luke, "The Photographic Reproduction of Space," 341. And Michael Diers's essay on the series of articles positions these debates as "Prolegomena" to the Benjamin essay, whose author himself locates conceptual antecedents in a 1930 talk with Adrien Monnier (simultaneous, Diers notes, with the facsimile debates in Germany). Michael Diers, "Kunst und Reproduktion: Der Hamburger Faksimile-Streit. Zum Wiederabdruck eines unbekannt gebliebenen Panofsky-Aufsatzes von 1930," *IDEA: Jahrbuch der Hamburger Kunsthalle* 5 (1986): 125–37.

[36] Benjamin, "The Work of Art," 24. This emancipation included freedom from "the criterion of authenticity" in application to art—allowing its "social function to become less one of ritual and instead one more vested in politics. Ibid., 25.

[37] "Das Problem der Kunstreproduktion wie der Kunstrestaurierung ist, wie überhaupt alles, eine Frage der Wahrheit und Echtheit." Eberlein, "Zur Frage," 652.

[38] For a comparison of Benjamin's and Einstein's perspectives on reproduction and repetition in particular, see Charles W. Haxthausen, "Reproduction/Repetition: Walter Benjamin/Carl Einstein," *October* 107 (Winter 2004): 47–74.

[39] "Wer das Faksimile verbietet, muß auch den Film, das Radio und das Grammophon verbieten. Denn es sind nah verwandte Dinge." Alexander Dorner, "Das Lebensrecht des Faksimiles," in *Beilage zum Hannoverschen Kurier* 264/265, June 9, 1929.

[40] "Aber wer wird heute noch wagen, zu sagen, ihm gehe der 'Schauer vor dem Kunstwerk' verloren, weil er Beethovens C-Moll Symphonie nicht im gedrängten Konzertsalle mit sichtbaren und unsichtbaren Störungen und in meist nicht einmal erstklassiger Aufführung im Original sieht, sondern 'nur' in der Reproduktion mit Hilfe eines vollwertigen Grammophons hört, und zwar wirklich in stiller Stunde." Ibid. Dorner's interest in augmenting visitor experience through reproductive apparatuses did not end with the cast or photographic replica but also extended to the gramophone. In his later work at the Museum of Art in Providence (1938–41), Dorner conceived of devices embedded in furniture that would play period music in the museum galleries.

[41] Panofsky, "Original and Facsimile Reproduction," 332; italics in the original.

[42] Alexander Dorner, "Original and Facsimile," 153.

[43] "Ich halte das Faksimile für ebenso falsch und verwerflich wie etwa den farbig bemalten Gipsabguss. . . ." Letter, Sauerlandt to Dorner, Hauptstaatsarchiv Hannover V.V.P. 21 Nr. 175.

[44] Panofsky, "Original and Facsimile Reproduction," 334.

[45] Küthmann and Noack hailed from the Kestner Museum in Hanover and the Städtische Sammlungen in Freiburg, respectively.

[46] "Ich darf vielleicht auch bemerken, dass ich ein paar Fragen zur Feststellung von Übermalungen auf alten Originalgemälden entdeckt habe, was immerhin Interesse und Verständnis für die Ziele Ihrer Vereinigung bekundet." Letter dated September 12, 1929. Hauptstaatsarchiv Hannover V.V.P. 21, no. 175. Dorner's tone continued in this vein throughout this correspondence—by November 1929 he attempted a comprehensive defense "so that my conscience is clear in this matter from A to Z" ("dass mein Gewissen in dieser Sache von A–Z rein ist"), which seemingly did little to alter Sauerlandt's opinion. Dorner to Sauerlandt, letter, November 13, 1929, Zentralarchiv, Staatliche Museen zu Berlin, III/DMB 301.

[47] "Verhandlungen der fünfundzwanzigsten Versammlung des Verbandes von Museumsbeamten zur Abwehr von Fälschungen und unlauterem Geschäftsgebaren," minutes of the twenty-fifth meeting of the Association of Museum Officials, Leipzig, September 23 and 24, 1929, 4: http://digiview.gbv.de/viewer/image/PPN616566166_1929/4/.

[48] Carl Georg Heise, *Der Gegenwärtige Augenblick: Reden und Aufsätze aus vier Jahrzenten* (Berlin: Gebr. Mann Verlag, 1960), 169. Also cited in Diers, "Kunst und Reproduktion," 127.

[49] The association did, however, take a position supporting "respect for the uniqueness of the original," according to a letter from Sauerlandt to Dorner of September 5, 1929. See Monika Flacke-Knoch, *Museumskonzeptionen in der Weimarer Republik: Die Tätigkeit Alexander Dorners im Provinzialmuseum Hannover* (Marburg: Jonas Verlag für Kunst und Literatur, 1985), 105. Flacke-Knoch's extensive handling of the Sauerlandt–Dorner correspondence positions these two characters as marking the "two completely opposite positions that marked the museum landscape of the 1920s." Ibid., 110.

[50] These articles appeared respectively in *Kunst und Künstler* 7 (1928): 251; 3 (1929): 109; and 8 (1929): 326.

[51] "Tagung des Deutschen Museumsbundes in Essen," in *Essen Volkszeitung*, August 21, 1930. Compiled in series in "*Original und Reproduktion,* Ausstellung im Museum Folkwang (14.09–12.10.1930) & Tagung des Deutschen Museumsbundes in Essen (14.–16.09.1930)." Supplied by Stadtarchiv Essen—Haus der Essener Geschichte, courtesy of Hans-Jürgen Lechtreck.

[52] In "'Original und Reproduktion' im Folkwang-Museum," *Essen Volkszeitung*, September 17, 1930. Supplied by Stadtarchiv Essen—Haus der Essener Geschichte, courtesy of Hans-Jürgen Lechtreck.

[53] Diers, "Kunst und Reproduktion," 128–29.

[54] "Protokoll der Tagung der Abteilung A (Kunst und Kulturmuseen in Essen) am 14. und 15. Sept. 1930," in Zentralarchiv, Staatliche Museen zu Berlin: III/DMB 003.

55 Pip Laurenson, "Authenticity, Change, and Loss in the Conservation of Time-Based Media Installations." Tate Papers, 2006. Available at http://www.tate.org .uk/research/publications/tate-papers/authenticity-change-and-loss-conservation -time-based-media.

56 Ibid.

57 "Is the post-loss state the same as pre-loss state? Does the hand of another change the authenticity or 'aura' of the art?" Renée Vara, "Valuation Determination & Damage in Contemporary Art," paper presented at The First Crack: A Symposium on Conservation and Value in Contemporary Art, hosted by Contemporary Conservation Ltd. and the School of Visual Arts, New York, April 2015.

Don't Let War Plants Scare You

By LOUIS KAHN[1]

A MAN who designed many of them tells why arms factories will play but little part in postwar civilian industry

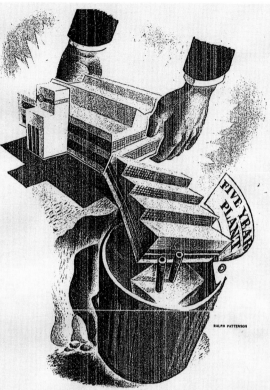

RALPH PATTERSON

Knowing that many facilities now being used will be obsolete in five years, wise companies are already drawing building plans

WHEN peace comes and America's war factories become available for turning out civilian goods, will we not have a tremendous excess of industrial plants?

The answer, though many-sided, is emphatically *no*.

America, as a matter of fact, faces an immediate postwar shortage, rather than a saturation, of production facilities.

This does not mean that our war plants are inefficient. They are entirely adequate for the war jobs for which they were designed.

But many are simply not convertible —except at excessive cost—to civilian production. These were built for a specific type of product, and when they have served their purpose, they are through. This is particularly true of many plants built since the spring of 1942.

An acutely critical situation in structural steel, copper for fittings, and other vital war materials radically changed the basic plan of many war plants. Alternate materials were used wherever possible, and new architectural design and structural methods had to be invented to circumvent the material prohibitions.

Far-sighted officials in the armed forces and government agencies, recog-

[1]President, Albert Kahn Associated Architects & Engineers, Inc. This firm designed and supervised the construction of Ford Willow Run, Chrysler Tank Arsenal, Hudson Naval Ordnance Plant, Higgins-New Orleans, Dodge-Chicago (largest industrial layout in the world), numerous Curtis-Wright plants and many other important projects.

nizing the doubtful postwar value of plants built for heavy war material, determined on semipermanent structures. "Five-year plants," we called them, because, at the time they were built, five years was the maximum productive life expected of them.

Too costly for part time

IN designing these plants, every possible short cut was taken to save time, costs and materials and still have plants entirely adequate for their intended job. They were "streamlined" to the ultimate degree. An example is lighting. We knew that the plant would operate around the clock, on an all-out basis, so there was no need to take the time and materials to wire each individual bay for lighting. Whole departments were hooked up to one master switch.

The effect is the same as though, coming home at night, you pressed the switch inside the front door and lighted your entire house. This method saved installation time and materials. It saved the time of operators, who could light the plant by pulling several master switches instead of many hundreds.

Yet, if such a plant were to be operated on a reduced production schedule, under private ownership, it would have to be completely rewired. Otherwise the power wastage would be a forbidding cost item.

As with lighting, so alterations would have to be made with materials-handling devices, heating, ventilation, layout and many other factors entering into the cost of civilian production.

What utility some of these "five-year plants" will have after the war is problematical. Some probably will be razed. This may sound like waste. But all war is waste. Those who were privileged to work with government officials are convinced that the undramatic story of vision and good sense in building for

(Continued on page 70)

---

1. Ralph Patterson, "Five Year Plant," 1944. In Louis Kahn, "Don't Let War Plants Scare You," *Nation's Business* 32 (1944): 28.

Adam Lauder and Lee Rodney

Albert Kahn's Five-Year Plant and the Birth of "Uncertain Space"

Two hands thrust a cutting-edge factory complex into an over-sized dustbin in a ludicrously self-reflexive image from an April 1944 *Nation's Business* article (Figure 1).[1] The factory, perhaps intended to represent an architect's model, sports the curious label "Five Year Plant." The author, Louis Kahn (no relation to Louis I. Kahn), was then president of the Detroit-based firm of Albert Kahn Associated Architects and Engineers, Inc., one of the most prolific architectural actors of the twentieth century and the originator of the "semipermanent" building type illustrated by Ralph Patterson.[2] "'Five-year plants,' we called them," Kahn explains; "because, at the time they were built, five years was the maximum productive life expected of them."[3] Writing more than a year prior to the cessation of hostilities about a building type that had only premiered in spring 1942, Kahn was already confronting its obsolescence (Figure 2): "Many are simply not convertible—except at excessive cost—to civilian production. These were built for a specific type of product, and when they have served their purpose, they are through."[4]

The economic implications of this new form of "emergency building" are staggering: construction contracts under the war program—many of them for plants of this disposable type—in 37 eastern states in 1942 alone totaled $8,255,000,000 (in 1942 U.S. currency).[5] The five-year plant was a lesser-known—but no less influential for that—invention of the company that is often subsumed under the authorship of the eponymous Albert Kahn (1869–1942), Louis's brother. Kahn is chiefly remembered for its partnership with Ford Motor Company in developing important early mass-production facilities, including Highland Park (1909), where the assembly line was introduced beginning in 1913 (Figure 3), and River Rouge (1917–1928), where it was subsequently perfected.

Although the modernist valorization of innovation has predictably meant that these earlier structures have received the lion's share of scholarly attention devoted to Kahn, this article shifts the focus onto the unique features of the five-year plant in order to situate it within the emergence of what French spatial theorist Henri Lefebvre (1901–1991) termed "abstract space."[6] Kahn's five-year plants instantiate an emergent logic of "uncertainty" that is also legible in the contemporaneous models of classical information theory and the dynamics of emergency management informing present-day preservation

Future Anterior
Volume XII, Number 2
Winter 2015

Don't Let War Plants Scare You

Peace will bring demands for new, practical buildings for specific purposes

(Continued from page 27)
production will prove one of the most effective phases of the entire war effort.

Of the war plants built for permanency, some undoubtedly will remain in government control on curtailed production or on experiment and research. Only an extreme pacifist would argue that America will again convert all its swords into plowshares.

Some plants now on war production will, of course, turn to producing for the civilian economy. This is indicated particularly in the aluminum, magnesium and synthetic rubber industries. Yet, those industries were volume producers before the war only to a degree and what they produce for civilian use will be new production, superimposed on our prewar economy.

While there is controversy over the future of synthetic rubber in America, it would seem simple good sense to keep that industry active, and the labor of producing rubber in American workmen's hands, at least through the immediate postwar adjustment period.

Small competition in space

IT SEEMS likely, however, that the total amount of war-plant floor space likely to compete with the tremendous going production plant of America will be small.

Because of the dramatic emphasis on war plants, many people assume they comprise a much larger share of our total factory area than is actually the case. While exactly comparable figures are not available, the War Production Board, reporting on the distribution of government contracts for war supplies, industrial plant and equipment from June, 1940, to June, 1943, set the amount at $14,515,000,000. This includes the cost of land, construction and equipment for industrial facilities.

The National Industrial Conference Board lists the national inventory of machinery, plant and other operating facilities in 1940 at $52,800,000,000. This total does not include cost of land and some related non-production facilities which are part of the $14,515,000,000 government total.

It is obvious from these figures that government war plants thus amount to approximately 25 per cent of our going civilian production capacity. Economists say we must, and can, double our prewar production output, which implies a much greater increase in production facilities than 25 per cent.

Yet, even this 25 per cent embodies those plants of exclusive wartime utility, including some of the largest individual layouts in the emergency building program. They are not adaptable to civilian production, will not be converted. Likewise, a large number of "five-year plants" must be deducted. So must those which will remain under government control.

What remains for possible civilian conversion is insignificant in relation to our total production plant.

As an offset to this small increase are those plants which were producing before the war but will not again build civilian goods because of obsolescence.

A sufficient answer to the entire question of the effect of war-plants on postwar manufacture, it seems to me, is the fact that practical industrialists are now ordering plans for new plants to be built as quickly as possible after the war ends.

In support of their judgment, based on their own individual company outlook, is the record of building generally. Building contract awards disclose that, in the '30's, construction of all types was only fractionally that of the '20's.

In 37 eastern states in 1928, the prewar peak year of building, construction in all categories—commercial, industrial, residential, public works, and utilities—totalled $6,628,000,000. This was only slightly larger than in 1927, and was not again realized even in 1941 when contracts already being let for war plants pushed the total to $6,007,000,000.

By 1942, under the full impetus of the war program, the total soared to $8,255,000,000, about one-third larger than the annual average in 1927-'29.

If the rate of building in 1942 was sustained in 1943, which does not appear probable, we will have accumulated a two-year bulge of less than $4,000,000,000 to apply against a continuous annual deficit since 1929 in normal construction.

Everywhere you look, new industrial plants will be needed.

This is necessary work—work dictated by the profit motive. Modern production managers know they can no more compete in obsolete plant housing than a motor freight carrier could operate profitably with old equipment.

Industrialists will spend money for new construction because they know they will more than get it back in low-cost selling. If this seems a crass frame for a roseate picture of postwar America, it is nothing to be ashamed of. The profit motive is the very epitome of the American system of free enterprise at its functional best.

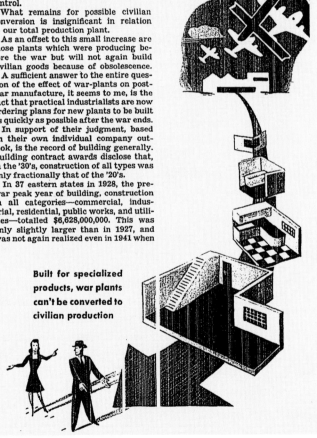

Built for specialized products, war plants can't be converted to civilian production

3. Albert Kahn, Inc., Original Building, Highland Park Plant, Highland Park, Michigan, 1909. Photograph courtesy of Albert Kahn Family of Companies.

initiatives in Detroit. The principles of efficiency, flexibility, and disposability built into Kahn's shed-like five-year plants recall the "uncertain" space of classical information theory. While filling lacunae in Lefebvre's historicization of abstract space, the isomorphic models of Kahn and Claude Shannon (1916–2001) also add new complexities to the French theorist's descriptions of "contradictory space."

The surge of media interest in Detroit over the past decade is arguably linked to larger discussions on precarity and emergency management. Franco Berardi defines precarity as "the area of work which is no longer defined by fixed rules relative to the labour relation, to salary, and to the length of the day."[7] Angela Mitropoulos recognizes troubling homologies between the differentiated composition of the precariat and the constitutive plurality of post-Fordist markets.[8] Similar tensions can be seen to characterize the dynamics of what Naomi Klein has provocatively dubbed "disaster capitalism," a formation mobilized by the "treatment of disasters as exciting market opportunities."[9] Kahn's five-year plants were early manifestations of this logic of emergency planning, which is not merely a product of the 2008 economic crisis but part of a longer arc of planning logic that brought about flexible and uncertain spaces as a key feature of modernity, informed by capitalism's experimentation with planned obsolescence and creative destruction.[10] That Kahn's firm established itself in Detroit during the height of the city's growth in the 1910s and 1920s suggests that the flexible spaces that Kahn designed for manufacturing were later refined and perfected in the five-year factories that his company developed during Detroit's phase as the Arsenal of Democracy in World War II.

As precarity is both a symptom of and catalyst for recent neoliberal economic imperatives, looking at Kahn's five-year plants complicates our understanding of the last economic crisis and its implications for architectural preservation. These offer a view to the built environment that embeds precarity as a longstanding phenomenon, one that does not directly follow the more recent economic trajectory from Keynesian to neoliberal policy that has been playing out since the 1980s. In considering the fate of the Willow Run Bomber Plant, for example, it is possible to read an emergency logic in the "intersections between super-profits and mega disasters" that has been developing for some time.[11]

This research builds on the insights of urban historians and geographers who have traced the dispersion of American cities after World War II as planning exercises that were based on forms of emergency management.[12] While it is well known that Fordism precipitated a move away from urban density, military-planning imperatives accelerated and justified Ford's early twentieth-century move away from the city, with Kahn following suit at River Rouge and later at Willow Run. Jennifer Light notes that the logic of national security, which began to inform urban planning in the 1940s, was underwritten by "an older way of thinking about civilian protection—that once again, urban designs would have to place fear of military attack front and center."[13] We are currently no strangers to the logic of fear that governs contemporary urban development and preservation. It is at work in the "risk society" of contemporary security discourse and in the "state of exception" that mutually underpins the perpetual war on terror and the dismantling of the welfare state through neoliberal economics.[14] However familiar this discourse of fear is in contemporary culture, it correlates with emergent mid-twentieth-century ideas that were manifest in Kahn's five-year plants.

As Detroit undergoes its most recent phase of urban renewal, which has at its base extensive plans for the demolition of abandoned housing and other buildings, the balance between downsizing and preservation has become a critical focus. The 2012 Detroit Works Project's "Rightsizing" campaign has aimed to provide a framework for the city in its current postbankruptcy phase, as a longstanding backlog of unpaid property taxes has left many neighborhoods without basic services such as electricity and water.[15] While the plan directs scant city resources toward areas such as Downtown and Mid-town Detroit, as well as other areas that are rapidly redeveloping, questions remain as to what options are available for those left living in unserviced parts of the city. Thus far, most of Detroit's success stories in the media have been linked to an idea of preservation that is informed by large-scale renewal projects that are connected to the rhetoric of creative economies, repurposing space for entertainment, and "new jobs" that are distinctly distanced from the prewar notions of labor that still shapes Detroit's sprawling urban imprint.

Abstract Space and Fordism

The Production of Space (1974) presents both a theory of how spaces are produced through social practice as well as a history of the rise and fall of distinct spatial "codes" associated with successive modes of production: from Neolithic agriculture to contemporary neocapitalism.[16] Lefebvre's historicization of space hinges on the ascendance of what he terms abstract space: "Formal and quantitative," he writes, "it erases distinctions, as much those which derive from nature and (historical) time as those which originate in the body (age, sex, and ethnicity)."[17] Surprisingly, nowhere does Lefebvre discuss Henry Ford's influential assembly line in his analysis of how "labour fell prey to abstraction";[18] this despite the transformative impact of Fordism on mass production and the unprecedented degree of functionalism that it required in factory design. Perhaps reflecting his own European experience, Lefebvre chooses instead to highlight the role of the German Bauhaus and architects associated with the International Style such as Le Corbusier who played a critical role in the emergence of a newly "global concept of space"[19] suturing the industrial and domestic spheres within the homogeneous space of capital flows.

While the self-conscious minimalism of Mies van der Rohe undoubtedly came to stand for the eventual triumph of the machine aesthetic during the 1950s,[20] recent studies by David Gartman, Mauro Guillén, and Terry Smith, among others, emphasize the extent to which European architects mimicked the look of earlier American factory buildings — particularly those designed by Kahn. These scholars underscore the degree to which the novel character of modernist space was largely symbolic, where Kahn's buildings exemplified, to quote Terry Smith, "an architectural-engineering functionalism so total, so exact yet flexible, that it embodied in actuality the principles of architectural modernism that the European innovators and their American followers achieved only symbolically."[21] In some cases, this borrowing extended to outright appropriation, as in Mies van der Rohe's 1942 proposal for a concert hall (Figure 4), which transformed an uncredited photograph of a Kahn factory building — the 1937 Assembly Building of Glenn L. Martin Company Plant in Middle River, Maryland (Figure 5) — into a

4. Ludwig Mies van der Rohe, Project for Concert Hall, 1942. Collage over photograph, 75 x 157.5 cm, Museum of Modern Art, New York. Gift of Mary Callery. Copyright Estate of Ludwig Mies van der Rohe / SODRAC (2015); copyright ARS, NY. Digital Image copyright The Museum of Modern Art / Licensed by SCALA / Art Resource, N.Y.

photomontage whose supplementary, ahistorical elements bring into representation the logic of superficial aestheticization critiqued by Gartman and Guillén.[22]

By contrast with the symbolic approach to design adopted by European architects, Federico Bucci argues that Kahn's designs were direct expressions of the abstract qualities of Fordist space: "The economy of time and space, and the insistence upon cleanliness, lighting and ventilation — expressed with characteristic succinctness, these were the fundamental principles of the Fordist rationale of space."[23]

The purpose of shifting the focus of this discourse onto Kahn is not to perpetuate a modernist emphasis on "firsts" but rather to see what might be gained by grafting Kahn's Fordist "representations of space" onto the symbolic or "representational spaces" of the International Style to which Lefebvre assigns such a pivotal status in his account of the ascendancy of abstract space (to employ but two of the three elements comprising the spatial theorist's conceptual "triad").[24] While studies such as Martha Banta's *Taylored Lives* have begun to uncover the impact of Fordist instrumentalism on the lived experience of workers as well as the domestic sphere — where the techniques of scientific management that fueled Ford's innovations were imported by reformers such as Frank and Lillian Gilbreth — our discussion is focused on Lefebvre's representation/representational dyad.

But rather than emphasize, as previous studies invariably have done, Kahn's early designs for Ford's assembly-line plants, we trouble this logic of "firsts" by exploring the lesser-known series of buildings designed by Kahn's firm to support the American war effort in World War II, namely, the five-year plants. These were factories commissioned under such acute conditions of immediate need and uncertain future use that the "shed"-like schema of earlier factory buildings designed

5. Albert Kahn, Inc., Assembly Building, Glenn L. Martin Company Plant, Middle River, Maryland, 1937. Photograph courtesy of Albert Kahn Family of Companies.

by Kahn at River Rouge to accommodate continuous modifications in the production process were pushed to a new extreme, whereby the building became little more than a vast box: the precursor to the ubiquitous "big box" spaces of contemporary suburbia.[25] Daniel Abramson situates the emergence of such factories within an architectural genealogy of "obsolescence" defined by a conjunction of rhetoric and techniques aimed at "control[ling] capitalist crises through planning and regulation" in a fashion reminiscent of Joseph Schumpeter's description of capitalism as "creative destruction."[26]

Incorporating a study of Kahn's work within Lefebvre's historicizing account of abstract space adds further complexity to the history of multiple representations and their interrelationship that his text calls for.[27] The dissonant resonance of Kahn's uncertain spaces should be understood, then, as embodying the "contradictions"[28] of abstract space discussed by Lefebvre, rather than necessitating a new spatial category altogether.

If Kahn's early factory designs of the 1910s and 1920s can be said to embody a logic of movement suggesting analogies with the "movement-image"[29] that philosopher Gilles Deleuze posits as the basis of early moving-image technologies, but premised on Frederick Taylor's principles of scientific management, the architect's later five-year plants reflect a new engagement with problems of disposability and, especially, uncertainty that is also visible in the nearly contemporaneous rhetoric of information theory.

Kahn's Collaborative Production

Although studies have tended to focus on the leadership of Albert Kahn within the various iterations of his firm, buildings designed by his office were very much corporate efforts.[30] Chris Meister goes furthest in stressing the formative role of Kahn's brothers, especially Julius—an engineer and founder of the Trussed Concrete Steel Company[31]—not only in the administrative affairs of the firm but in contributing directly to the company's structural innovations, the decisive role of Julius's patented "Kahn Bar" in its celebrated use of reinforced concrete at Packard Number Ten and other early projects being a striking case in point.[32] Moritz Kahn's supervision of the Moscow division of Albert Kahn, Inc., from 1928 to 1932—a remarkable venture in transnational exchange that resulted in the construction of 521 plants in the U.S.S.R. and the training of more than 4,000 Soviet engineers and other personnel[33]— is another impressive instance of this corporate model, for which Albert Kahn's notorious claim that "Industrial Architecture today is about 90% Business and 10% Art" is an apt description.[34]

It is more than this collaborative dimension of the Kahn office that troubles romantic models of authorship, however. As Charles Hyde has noted, as early as 1905—more then eight years prior to Ford's introduction of the moving assembly line into automotive production at the Highland Park plant—Kahn rationalized his office's workflows, in effect "creating an architectural assembly line."[35] In sharp contrast to the romanticized personae cultivated by contemporaries such as Le Corbusier and Frank Lloyd Wright, the collective and rationalized working methods adopted by Kahn's firm (which Bucci attributes to Albert's brothers Louis and Moritz)[36] laid the groundwork for the integration of architectural and engineering specialists seen in later firms such as Skidmore, Owings and Merrill.[37] It is tempting to postulate Kahn's streamlining of architectural practice along assembly-line principles as a direct, if subterranean influence on Ford's innovations, as Federico Bucci,[38] Grant Hildebrand, and Terry Smith have all suggested. Smith argues that "[Kahn's] office became part of the team, orchestrated by Ford, which *invented* line production."[39] While for the sake of convenience this article makes frequent reference to Albert Kahn in the singular, Kahn's authorship was collective and transdisciplinary.

Information Theory, the "Conduit Metaphor," and Spaces of Uncertainty

Louis Cohen situates the militarized spaces of Kahn and other wartime architects against a backdrop in which "information was ever-present."[40] But whereas Cohen's study focuses on the representational role of information deployed during World War II in the service of strategy, surveillance, and tactics—from camouflage to simulation—this essay will explore structural parallels between the "tendency towards uniformity" exhibited by Kahn's five-year plants and the nascent space of information theory as a measure of uncertainty.[41]

Like Kahn's five-year plant, information theory was a by-product of war. Its chief architect, Claude Shannon, developed the principles of information theory out of classified work conducted at Bell Telephone Labs on the "X System" for encrypting communications between Franklin D. Roosevelt and Winston Churchill during World War II.[42] While contributing to this project in New York City in 1943, Shannon came into contact with British mathematician Alan Turing (1912–1954), who shared the legendary paper he had published seven years earlier, "On Computable Numbers," that laid the groundwork for modern computation.[43] Shannon initially synthesized his wartime insights on communication in a classified 1945 memorandum for Bell Labs, later declassified and published in the *Bell System Technical Journal* as the influential 1949 article "A Mathematical Theory of Communication." While the manifold implications of Shannon's theory of communication are too complex to address in any detail here, there are two concepts we will highlight by way of proposing a bridge with Kahn's five-year plants and the logic of state violence that precipitates abstract space in Lefebvre's account.

Information studies scholar Ronald Day argues that Shannon's ubiquitous diagram (Figure 6) of the communication process—which depicts messages sent by a transmitter traveling through a linear channel to be received by a "destination" at the other end—circulated as a metaphor with "tremendous cultural and social importance" throughout the Cold War period.[44] Dubbed the "conduit metaphor" by Michael J. Reddy, Shannon's transportation model of communication has been linked to both cybernetic systems of command and control,[45] as well as an emergent global space of "networks" associated with the rise of what Michael Hardt and Antonio Negri characterize as a society defined by processes of "informatization."[46] While it is easy enough to see how the branching lines of Shannon's conduit form the basic unit of a networked space,[47] the conduit itself, and the empty boxes in which information is transmitted and received, demand further reflection upon how these cellular units function as *spaces*.

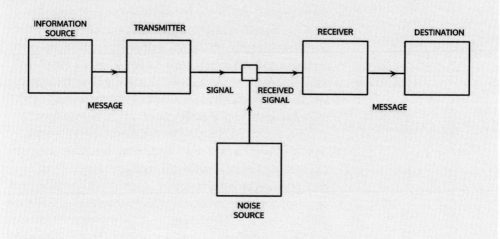

6. Claude E. Shannon, "Schematic diagram of a general communication system," 1949.

Before grappling with this problem, we must first come to terms with a second conceptual legacy of Shannon's theory with direct implications for Kahn's five-year plants and Lefebvre's abstract space, namely, its redescription of communication as nonsemantic "information" and, in turn, its definition of information as the mathematical measure of *uncertainty,* or, the degree of "freedom" or "choice" between multiple possible messages sent or received.[48] In Shannon's counterintuitive formulation, as uncertainty increases—as more "noise" interferes with the message—information content increases proportionally. This element of indeterminacy at the heart of Shannon's information theory is frequently overlooked by commentators overeager to peg information theory as a monolithic instrument of normative control.

As previously noted, the theory's origins in wartime cryptography and, later, in Bell Telephone's proprietary communications networks irrevocably align Shannon's theory with Lefebvre's descriptions of abstract space as profoundly implicated in the exercise of state violence and neocapitalist networks. However, it is important to underline the residual possibility for transformation and resistance implied by the element of "choice" between multiple messages that remains a perpetual resource to the user in this schema, and, as communications scholar Gary Genosko argues in his reevaluation of the metaphor of the "telegraph girl" deployed by Warren Weaver in his postwar popularization of Shannon's theory,[49] to the operator of the channel (be it human or nonhuman).

Why this detour through Shannon's definition of information as probability or uncertainty? Considered as a channel first and foremost, the theorist's highly indeterminate schematization of information has important implications for the space of the conduit, which, prior to being one branch in a global network, must first be understood as a *space of uncertainty.* Unlike the metaphor of the obscuring "black box" harnessed by French sociologist of science Bruno Latour to critique scientific statements — a box that obfuscates the socially situated and contingent workings of "science in action" by reducing it to a repeatable "input" and "output" of data[50] — the space of Shannon's conduit incorporates the potentially transformational force of information as "choice" or "freedom," or what Day terms "good information" — as opposed to the "bad information" of cybernetic control.[51]

As a measure of what messages can *come to be,* Shannon's formula for measuring the capacity of a given information channel acquires an ontological value that resonates with the ontological turn in Edward Soja's Marxist geography: a radical rethinking of earlier accounts of the space of "dwelling" elaborated by Heidegger and Sartre.[52]

Something akin to this ontological principle is at work in Kahn's five-year plant, which, though deployed in the service of a destructive war economy, nonetheless incorporates within itself at least a latent possibility for transformation that answers Lefebvre's characterization of the "contradictory" nature of abstract space. Here, lurking within the very crucibles of the contemporary regime of space — the wellsprings of abstract labor, communication, and warfare — is embedded a *marge de manoeuvre* that somewhat contradicts the logic of control imputed by Lefebvre to neocapitalist space, its representations and representational symbols, thereby offering something of a working model of the spatial theorist's notion of contradictory space as the precondition for an emergent "differential" or counterspace.[53]

Willow Run

Reading Kahn's five-year plant as a representation of Lefebvrian abstract space calls for a careful analysis of a concrete example of this building type. Such a reading poses a number of difficulties due to the relative paucity of published material devoted to these ephemeral, and at one time mostly classified, structures. Although Louis Kahn's 1944 article on the five-year plant does not identify any specific examples of this building type — cryptically conflating it with "war factories" designed by his company, particularly those after 1942 — some measure of its ubiquity is suggested by Kahn's accounting. He estimated that war factories represented one quarter of all production

7. Photograph of a Scale Model of
the Willow Run Bomber Plant, 1941.
Courtesy The Henry Ford Museum.
P.833.75904.

facilities constructed in the United States between June 1940
and June 1943, or, approximately $14,515,000,000 in govern-
ment contracts.[54] One exception to this amnesia stands out:
the Willow Run manufacturing complex (Figure 7), located
between Ypsilanti and Belleville, Michigan — just beyond the
suburban belt of contemporary Detroit. This plant has gener-
ated a comparative wealth of commentary since its construction in 1942, a fact that likely reflects both the unprecedented
scale of the structure — at the time of its construction, the
largest industrial building ever designed — as well as its propagandistic function during wartime. Warren Kidder argues that,
"after Pearl Harbor, it was Willow Run that excited the nation.
Willow Run and Henry Ford became a rallying point of hope
against the Japanese."[55] This propagandistic dimension of the
complex underlines the dual character of the five-year plant as
both what Lefebvre would term "representation" (functional)
and "representational" (symbolic) space.

The sheer speed with which Willow Run was planned and
constructed speaks to the fundamentally "uncertain" character
of the five-year plant. In his memoir, Executive Vice-President
of Ford Motor Company Charles E. Sorensen recalled that
"our organization moved fast — and dangerously" to construct
Willow Run.[56] Amazingly, it was a mere nineteen months from
authorization to the completion of this unprecedented facility.[57]

This compressed timeline, compounded by the colossal scale of the factory, necessitated an unparalleled coordination of labor, parts, and schedules. Kidder reports that, as of September 17, 1941, the project's payroll included 2,909 employees: almost 2,200 of whom were involved in construction of the factory itself.[58] These personnel problems were exacerbated by both an acute lack of worker housing as well as an inadequate supply of experienced aircraft workers.[59] The latter problem required training more than 50,000 civilian laborers and 20,000 soldiers in less than three years.[60]

Compounding these uncertainties would have been the fact that Kahn's firm — accustomed to working in close collaboration with clients and their engineers to tailor specifications to particular production processes — is likely to have received scant information from either Ford or the U.S. Government. Writing about the slightly earlier Chrysler Tank Arsenal in Detroit (1941), Hildebrand states that, "in the end [the client's] criteria were, no doubt, vague, and Kahn was probably instructed to design a plant with maximum flexibility and minimal foreseeable obstructions; in any event this is what he did. [. . .] The plan is thus an *abstraction* of the rudiments of manufacture."[61] Kahn's five-year plants bring into representation Hildebrand's thesis that the architect's later buildings evince a growing formulaic tendency that distinguishes them from the always-contingent character of his River Rouge designs of the 1920s.[62] For Hildebrand, Kahn's "style" paradoxically lies in this reduction of aesthetic problems to a flexible "vocabulary" of functional solutions;[63] a formulation that resonates with Abramson's description of the "shed-type factory" as a highly ambivalent adaptation to the contradictory pressures of obsolescence.[64]

When considering these factors as evidence of the newly "uncertain" character of the five-year plant, it is germane to place them within the context of Kahn's concurrent projects. Hildebrand states that, "from December 1939 to December 1942 the government alone commissioned the office to design $200 million worth of construction, and until at least December 1941 this was supplemented by the usual volume of work from private industry."[65] While the proverbial condition of "information overload" wrought by the novel challenges posed by Willow Run in itself attests to the acute forces of uncertainty that shaped Kahn's spaces during this period, when set within the context of the firm's greater wartime efforts the situation begins to appear more like the chaotic cosmos theorized contemporaneously by the field of quantum mechanics.[66]

Recalling Kahn's earlier reorganization of his own office along assembly-line principles, Kidder states that "the task of setting up production at Willow Run was like a factory itself—

the largest in the world."[67] Uncertainty was not confined to logistics: the architecture and layout of the plant had to be improvised in a fashion that Kahn's earlier designs for the River Rouge plant never were.[68] The first sketch for what was to become Willow Run was drafted by Sorensen on the night of January 8, 1941, *prior* to consultation with Kahn's firm, following the former's tour of Consolidated Aircraft in San Diego: the developer of the B-24.[69] "I'll have something for you tomorrow morning, I said [to the Consolidated Aircraft people]." Sorensen later recalled: "I was back to my old game of sketching a series of manufacturing and assembly operations and their orderly progression toward becoming major units—a game I had played many times since that morning in 1908 at the Piquette Avenue plant when we first experimented with a moving assembly line."[70] The uncompromising minimalism of the resulting "L"-shaped megastructure exemplifies Louis Kahn's subsequent description of the five-year plants:[71]

> They were "streamlined" to the ultimate degree. An example is lighting. We knew that each plant would operate around the clock, on an all-out basis, so there was no need to take the time and materials to wire each individual bay for lighting. Whole departments were hooked up to one master switch.[72]

Working from a scale model of the monumental factory, Ford's Layout Department devised the placement of machinery while the plant was still being built. This procedure marked a decisive departure from the methods followed by Ford and Kahn since at least the "New Plant" at Highland Park, for which Sorensen later claimed that Ford's chief construction engineer, Edward Grey, supplied volume calculations and floor plans, Kahn merely producing an architectural "envelope" *ex post facto.*[73] By contrast, during the construction of Willow Run, staff in Ford's Layout Department worked on fiberboards— each representing one fifty-seventh of the assembly area—to place equipment in a pregiven container. While the technique of dividing the area of the factory model into modular units— subsequently photostated for reference during installation— might initially recall Lefebvre's characterization of abstract space as "formal and quantitative," as we have shown, nearly every element of the planning process for Willow Run implied a degree of uncertainty that renders the plant's resulting representation of space closer to Lefebvre's notion of an emergent "contradictory space."

The degree of uncertainty involved in the planning activities carried out by Ford's Layout Department appears in a wholly different perspective when it is realized that the mass-assembly of aircraft had never before been attempted. "When the government accepted Ford's proposal," Kidder writes, "it introduced into the aircraft industry two discordant systems of production, the unit production of the aircraft industry and the mass production methods of the automobile industry."[74] Synchronizing these divergent manufacturing systems required ad hoc testing of basic techniques (e.g., dies) and materials (aluminum).[75] Equally essential to the realization of this unprecedented synthesis of aviation and automotive methodologies was nothing less than "an entirely new type of plant."[76]

Inviting analogies with the linear "conduit" of Shannon's uncertain information space, Willow Run was initially conceived by Sorensen as a "mile long factory."[77] While Kahn's revised, L-shape design involved some modification to this scheme, the architect's description of it as "the most enormous room in the history of mankind"[78] corresponds with the stripped-down linearity of Shannon's diagram and its constituent "boxes." Designed by Albert Kahn Associates in less than two months, the factory floor covered 80.4 acres,[79] making it a giant box for processing uncertain processes that were, in a very concrete sense, still in-formation.

The location of the Willow Run complex, some thirty-five miles outside of Detroit, was not insignificant in terms of the logic of uncertainty underpinning the contradictory space suggested in the analogy with information theory. The temporary nature of the factory is underscored by two key decisions: the first, to locate the mammoth plant just beyond the boundaries of Washtenaw and Wayne counties, which were considered Democratic, union strongholds. The second critical decision, to discard various schemes for Bomber City, a proposed town center and urban development at the site, suggests the temporary nature of Willow Run. These plans were supported by the Roosevelt administration but ultimately rejected by Ford.[80] Additionally, the push toward decentralization in American cities was already gaining sway by the end of the War. The shift to the suburbs was most famously prophesied in the words of Ford himself, who announced in 1922 that "we shall solve the problem of the city by leaving the city," exiting Detroit to fully set up shop in Dearborn by the early 1920s. Willow Run followed in this gradual exodus from Detroit, but its plans differed significantly to project conditions of precariousness and uncertainty. Jean-Louis Cohen notes that the Willow Run complex was strategically located outside the town of Ypsilanti, far from existing housing (Detroit was then experiencing a now almost unimaginable shortage of housing at the time). Any plans for more permanent settlement were extinguished by the development of a three-level highway interchange system nearby that was part of a plan to bus workers in from outlying areas, while "complexes of huts, shacks, and even tents proliferated" near the Willow Run complex.[81] These details are in keeping with the strategic uncertainty suggested by the historical experiment in the mass assembly of aircraft that was undertaken at Willow Run in the 1940s, as well as the new conditions of labor that included mobile workforces (42,000 workers at the height of production) and women as temporary labor in the crisis economy of wartime production.

Crisis and "Presentism"

The various states of emergency of late—from the "war on terror" to the global economic crisis—have been sold to the public on the basis of exception: as temporary and necessary management strategies that will eventually cede a return to democratic process and civil liberties. However, it is also suggested that the many states of exception around the world have become the new normal, that emergency management forms the basis for contemporary politics.[82] Harry Harootunian has characterized the "endless war against terror" that defines our post-9/11 moment as installing a "perennial present" in which the "horizon of expectation" posited by German thinker Rheinhart Koselleck as the organizing topos of a post-Kantian subject that constructs its own historicity, is foreclosed in a permanent state of presentism that evacuates historical memory.[83] Harootunian compares and contrasts this contemporary process of dehistoricization with crises precipitated by World War II.

The two spaces that we have paired in this article likewise emerged out of the historical crisis of World War II, wherein even the "flexible" deadlines of just-in-time production had to be subsumed under a "disposable" future characterized by absolute uncertainty. This logic of presentism emerges with particular force from Bucci's discussion of Kahn's five-year plants as examples of what he terms "temporary architectures."[84] If the password "speed-speed-speed"[85] inscribed in these structures speaks to an emergent paradigm of "flexibility," as previously discussed in relation to Willow Run, they simultaneously bring into representation another dynamic of uncertainty linked to their disposability. While planned obsolescence was an anticipated feature of the five-year plant,[86] an unintended resonance with Harootunian's concept of presentism and the foreclosure of historical memory emerges from Kahn's earlier Rotunda Building (1934). Originally part of Ford's pavilion at the 1933 Chicago World Exhibition, it was subsequently dismantled and moved to the company's Dearborn headquarters, where—somewhat ironically, given its status as a so-called memory place—it was destroyed by fire soon afterward.[87]

Ralph Patterson's memorably paradoxical illustration of a five-year plant being tossed into the trash bin of history, introduced earlier, presents an even more poignant representation of the conflicting implications of presentism for Lefebvre's abstract space as expressing the internal "contradictions" of neocapitalism's deterritorializing flows of information and power. This image adds additional texture to Abramson's discussion of subsequent countercultural projects that seized upon the resistant potential of planned obsolescence, such as Archigram's disposable "Plug-in City" of 1962–66, or the flexible "Fun Palace" of Cedric Price (1961–64), as paradoxically originating "deep within the capitalist system."[88] We have already seen that Shannon's information space, with its always-negotiable content and disposable network of conduits, embodies allied pressures of accelerated circulation and persistent uncertainty. The spaces of Kahn and Shannon were products of the same "culture of control and subtle militarization" described by Cohen.[89] But the relatively greater elasticity and indeterminacy of Shannon's space invites analogies with the trash bin capable of consuming even the formidable dimensions of the five-year plant's shed-like space. Although it shows the two spaces to be contemporary, Patterson's prescient illustration suggests that an even more formless space—which we would now recognize as Shannon's conduit—stands poised, ouroboros-like, to devour Kahn's ephemeral plants. This emergent space of uncertainty or disaster constitutes the horizon of Abramson's paradigm of "sustainability" as the successor to planned obsolescence.

The uncertain spaces of Kahn and Shannon clear a path for the presentism of the contemporary moment—a moment defined by engineered crises and regimes of "disaster capitalism" (we need only think of recent events in Detroit, with its governor-appointed "emergency manager," Kevyn Orr). But the pairing of Kahn's five-year plant and Shannon's conduit in this article does not issue from any causal relationship between the two. Nevertheless, it is tempting to speculate on the possibility of an indirect influence exerted by Kahn's contributions to assembly-line production on a young Shannon, who was born in Michigan, and studied engineering at the University of Michigan—a campus dominated by buildings designed by Kahn, including his collaboration with George D. Mason on the 1903 Engineering Building—prior to doing graduate work at MIT with Vannevar Bush.[90] The recent work of Chris Meister has brought to light another connection between Kahn and the computing industry vis-à-vis the architect's longtime relationship with industrialist Joseph A. Boyer—proprietor of the Burroughs Adding Machine Company, subsequently a leading manufacturer of computers—whose 1904 American

Arithmometer Company Factory in Detroit involved the first application of the Kahn brothers' patented "Kahn System" of reinforced concrete.[91] Louis Kahn's role in designing strategic "information rooms" during World War II,[92] strengthens the probability of a direct exchange between the realms of information technology and architecture during the critical period of wartime crisis.

Whatever the case may be, our thesis is that Kahn's later buildings and Shannon's conduit reflect distinct but analogous responses to the crisis of modern warfare, which in turn both instantiate and add further texture to Lefebvre's descriptions of the history of representations as the history of "their relationships — with each other, with practice, and with ideology."[93]

Although Willow Run was conceived and built as a five-year factory to manufacture aircraft bombers, it ran for many years as General Motor's Powertrain plant, closing permanently only in 2010. As such, Willow Run was never disposed of in the manner prophesied by Ralph Patterson's dramatic illustration of 1944: the plant is only now being decommissioned by the RACER Trust (Revitalizing Auto Communities Environmental Response), as of 2013. In any case, the fantastical dustbin of history implied in the image of a disposable plant still functions as a powerful "representation of space" today. As the conceptual vacuum that conveniently cleans up the material remains of planned obsolescence, the metaphorical dustbin pictures flexibly in our current neoliberal crisis economy. It underwrites the ideals of economic growth and innovation, at the same time suggesting that capitalism only need deal with the environmental impact of manufacturing as a series of altruistic gestures. The RACER Trust was created in 2011 as part of General Motors Bankruptcy settlement following the financial crisis of 2008. It is charged with the "largest environmental response and remediation" in U.S. history, with Willow Run as the most significant site that the Trust is in charge of decommissioning and repurposing.[94]

However, a portion of Willow Run has been purchased to re-open the nearby Yankee Air Museum after it lost one of its hangars to fire in 2004. A popular fundraising campaign allowed the museum to purchase 175,000 square feet of the bomber plant from the RACER Trust to re-locate its collection and to frame it within the wartime ethos of the "Arsenal of Democracy." A major part of the fundraising campaign has focused on the story of "Rosie the Riveter" who was modeled after one of Willow Run's employees, Rose Will Monroe. Much is being made of this story through the museum's promotional website, where Rosie symbolizes a diversified and democratized workforce, while the factory itself is heralded as the birthplace of "just-in-time" manufacturing systems. These are hopeful statements after Detroit became the poster child for the 2008 recession, though they are also selective and partial readings of Willow Run's history as our reading of the uncertain space of this five-year plant has indicated above.

Conclusion

It is currently said that Detroit is now in a "post-post apocalyptic" phase, in the words of a recent piece in the *New York Times*.[95] The frequency with which Detroit features in news media around the world suggests that the city has become a favored symbol not only of the rise and fall of American manufacturing but of the vicissitudes of neoliberal economies more generally. In the latest chapter of Detroit's perpetual reinvention, led by the state-appointed Emergency Manager, Kevyn Orr, many of Detroit's formerly vacant commercial spaces are being recast as business "incubators" by Dan Gilbert, the founder and CEO of Quicken Loans. As a company that specializes in emergency finance and reverse mortgages, Gilbert has set up the company's corporate headquarters in a signature Albert Kahn Associates building from 1959, which has housed various financial institutions, from the National Bank of Detroit to J. P. Morgan Chase. In Gilbert's hands this modernist structure has been renamed the Qube, and its interior dramatically retrofitted in a neon palate with flexible workspaces that announce Quicken Loan's ascendancy in the world of creative finance.

The design of the retrofitted Kahn structure has been roundly criticized as tacky and garish, but it recalls key motifs of information theory, from the suggestion of digital noise conveyed by the pixilated patterning of the interior surfaces, to the linear "conduit" of Shannon's information space, discussed earlier in relation to Willow Run. In Gilbert's renovation of Kahn's structure, the uncertainty of Shannon's empty boxes return as break-out spaces, celebrated as signs of a triumphant flexibility and presentism.

In their unresolved tension between a functionalist representation of abstract space and the representational spaces of metaphor and symbolism, Shannon's "conduit" and Kahn's five-year plant emerge from this study as instantiating a shared mode of Lefebvrian contradictory space that we have termed "uncertain space," for the exceptional degree of "freedom" and disposability it embodies. While not yet satisfying Lefebvre's definition of a liberatory differential space, the foundational element of choice imbricated in this space spells the possibility of a new room to maneuver available for the user. Yet this essay has also underlined the extent to which the spaces of Kahn and Shannon are inextricably embedded in processes of state violence as well as the neocapitalist fragmentation of subjectivity and associated with the evacuation of history and foreclosure of futurity. These fault lines in uncertain space reveal at once its social constructedness and historicity as well as its potential for supporting resistant readings.

While the commercial structures of Willow Run and the Quicken Loans Headquarters are being retrofitted to keep pace with neoliberal values, it is important to note that counter-spaces have been proposed since the 1970s and continue to be tested in Detroit's vast inventory of abandoned domestic architecture. Camilo José Vergara's controversial proposal to make Detroit's abandoned skyscrapers into an "American acropolis," a museum of ruins at the centre of the city, calls into question how preservation activates memory.[96] Vergara's proposal proved to be too speculative to be taken seriously, as it posed too many difficult questions about the afterlife of architecture. But it is only now, after thirty or more years of vacancy, that Detroit's historic buildings are being considered for refurbishing. Programs like Brick + Beam provide a plat-form for "rehabbers" in Detroit to share resources and skills to help foster new projects and to keep existing ones moving along.[97] But there are also numerous projects at the level of the neighborhood or block that are being taken up as alternative modes of urban life.[98] While these spaces do not necessarily take a preservationist lead to restore what was once there, urban farms and intentional communities have been springing up in many parts of the city. These projects are informed by dif-ferent philosophies and levels of commitment, but in spite of their diversity the projects can be seen as united in their desire to redefine sustenance and sustainability. They also suggest something of the resistant potential implied by Lefebvre's read-ing of contradictory space as incubating the seeds of a counter-space. These trends have been developing now for nearly a decade. One hopes that in Detroit's recovery and "rightsizing" that the longer temporal horizons of preservation can maintain the contours of a complex urban history, while not falling prey to the same impulses that foreclosed on the city's recent past.

Biographies
Adam Lauder is a PhD candidate in the Department of Art at the University of Toronto.

Lee Rodney is associate professor of media art history and visual culture at the University of Windsor. Her forthcoming book, *Looking beyond Border Lines: North America's Frontier Imagination,* will be published in 2015.

Notes
[1] Louis Kahn, "Don't Let War Plants Scare You," *Nation's Business* 32 (1944): 27–28.
[2] Ibid., 27.
[3] Ibid.
[4] Ibid.
[5] Ibid., 28.

[6] Henri Lefebvre, *The Production of Space*, trans. Donald Nicholson-Smith (Malden, Mass.: Blackwell, 1991), 49.

[7] Franco Berardi, "Info Labour and Precariousness," generation-online.org, http://www.generation-online.org/t/tinfolabour.htm.

[8] Angela Mitropoulos, "Precari-Us?," eipcp, 2005, http://eipcp.net/transversal/0704/mitropoulos/en.

[9] Naomi Klein, *The Shock Doctrine: The Rise of Disaster Capitalism* (Toronto: Vintage Canada, 2007), 6.

[10] See Daniel M. Abramson, "From Obsolescence to Sustainability, Back Again, and Beyond," *Design and Culture* 4, no. 3 (2012): 279–98.

[11] Klein, *The Shock Doctrine*, 10.

[12] See Philipp Oswalt, ed., *Shrinking Cities* (Ostfildern-Ruit: Hatje Cantz, 2005).

[13] Jennifer Light, *From Warfare to Welfare: Defense Intellectuals and Urban Problems in Cold War America* (Baltimore: John Hopkins University Press, 2003), 15. See also Matthew Farish, "Disaster and Decentralization: American Cities and the Cold War," *Cultural Geographies* 10, no. 2 (2003): 125–48.

[14] See Giorgio Agamben, *State of Exception*, trans. Kevin Attell (Chicago: University of Chicago Press, 2005); Ulrich Beck, *Risk Society: Towards a New Modernity* (London: Sage, 1992).

[15] Brenna Moloney, *"Putting the Right in Rightsizing: A Historic Preservation Case Study,"* Michigan Historic Preservation Network and National Trust for Historic Preservation, 2012, http://preservationdetroit.org/preservation-advocacy/rightsizing/.

[16] Lefebvre, *The Production of Space*, 47.

[17] Ibid., 49.

[18] Ibid.

[19] Ibid., 124.

[20] David Gartman, *From Autos to Architecture: Fordism and Architectural Aesthetics in the Twentieth Century* (New York: Princeton Architectural Press, 2009), 13.

[21] Terry Smith, "Albert Kahn: High Modernism and Actual Functionalism," in *Albert Kahn: Inspiration for the Modern*, ed. Brian Carter, 28–40 (Ann Arbor: University of Michigan Museum of Art, 2001), 30.

[22] Brian Carter, "Kahn, Machines, and the Collapse of Boundaries," in *Albert Kahn: Inspiration for the Modern*, ed. Brian Carter, 42–52 (Ann Arbor: University of Michigan Museum of Art, 2001), 47.

[23] Federico Bucci, *Albert Kahn: Architect of Ford* (New York: Princeton Architectural Press, 2002), 41.

[24] See Lefebvre, *The Production of Space*, 38–39.

[25] "The use of large, windowless sheds, designed by American industry at the beginning of the war in a response to the blackout and the 24-hour production cycle, became widespread." Jean-Louis Cohen, *Architecture in Uniform: Designing and Building for the Second World War* (Montréal: Canadian Centre for Architecture; Paris: Hazan, 2011), 401.

[26] Daniel M. Abramson, "Obsolesence: Notes Towards a History," *Praxis* 5 (2003): 110; Abramson, "From Obsolescence to Sustainability," 281.

[27] "History," writes Lefebvre, "would have to take in not only the genesis of these spaces but also, and especially, their interconnections, distortions, displacements, mutual interactions, and their links with the spatial practice of the particular society or mode of production under consideration." Lefebvre, *The Production of Space*, 42.

[28] Ibid., 292.

[29] See Gilles Deleuze, *Cinema 1: The Movement-Image*, trans. Hugh Tomlinson and Barbara Habberjam (London: Athlone, 1986).

[30] Hildeband, *Designing for Industry*, 155.

[31] Chris Meister, "Albert Kahn's Partners in Industrial Architecture," *Journal of the Society of Architectural Historians* 72, no. 1 (2013): 81, 86.

[32] Meister, "Albert Kahn's Partners in Industrial Architecture," 85–92.

[33] Hildeband, *Designing for Industry*, 129.

[34] Albert Kahn, "Industrial Architecture: A Lecture by Albert Kahn," *Michigan Society of Architects* 13, no. 45 (1939): 8.

[35] Charles K. Hyde, "Assembly-Line Architecture: Albert Kahn and the Evolution of the U.S. Auto Factory," *The Journal of the Society for Industrial Archeology* 22, no. 2 (1996): 20.

[36] Bucci, *Albert Kahn*, 44–45, 129.

[37] Hyde, "Assembly-Line Architecture," 20.

[38] Bucci, *Albert Kahn*, 40, 123–35.

[39] Smith, "Albert Kahn," 39. Hildebrand similarly writes that "Kahn's office became a machine for the reproduction of mass production as a mode of industry." Hildeband, *Designing for Industry*, 39.

[40] Cohen, *Architecture in Uniform*, 321.

[41] Ibid., 14.

[42] James Gleick, *The Information: A History, A Theory, A Flood* (New York: Pantheon, 2011), 204.

[43] Ibid., 205.

[44] Ronald E. Day, "The 'Conduit Metaphor' and the Nature and Politics of Information Studies," *Journal of the American Society for Information Science* 51, no. 9 (2000): 807.

[45] Ronald E. Day, *The Modern Invention of Information: Discourses, History, and Power* (Carbondale: Southern Illinois University Press, 2001), 47–52.

[46] See Michael Hardt and Antonio Negri, "Postmodernization, or the Informatization of Production," in *Empire*, 280–303 (Cambridge, Mass.: Harvard University Press, 2000).

[47] See Mark Wigley, "Network Fever," *Grey Room*, no. 4 (2001): 82–122.

[48] Gleick, *The Information*, 219.

[49] Gary Genosko, *Remodelling Communication: From WWII to the WWW* (Toronto: University of Toronto Press, 2012), 36.

[50] Bruno Latour, *We Have Never Been Modern*, trans. Catherine Porter (Cambridge, Mass.: Harvard University Press, 1993), 24.

[51] Day, *The Modern Invention of Information*, 44.

[52] Edward W. Soja, *Postmodern Geographies: The Reassertion of Space in Critical Theory* (London: Verso, 1989), 131–37.

[53] Lefebvre, *The Production of Space*, 367.

[54] Kahn, "Don't Let War Plants Scare You," 28.

[55] Warren B. Kidder, *Willow Run: Colossus of American Industry* (Lansing, Mich.: s.n., 1995), 51, 55.

[56] Charles E. Sorensen, *My Forty Years with Ford* (Detroit, Mich.: Wayne State University Press, 2006), 276.

[57] Kidder, *Willow Run*, 68.

[58] Ibid., 98.

[59] Ibid., 58.

[60] Ibid., 130.

[61] Hildeband, *Designing for Industry*, 198–203; emphasis added.

[62] See ibid., 164–65.

[63] Ibid., 164.

[64] Abramson, "From Obsolescence to Sustainability," 283.

[65] Hildeband, *Designing for Industry*, 197.

[66] We want to thank Professor SeungJung Kim for her suggestion that the uncertain spaces of Kahn and Shannon bear a resemblance to Heisenberg's uncertainty principle. See also James Gleick's discussion of the influence of Heisenberg's concept on the work of Turing. Gleick, *The Information*, 212.

[67] Kidder, *Willow Run*, 137.

[68] Describing Kahn's 1922 Glass Plant for River Rouge complex as "the prototype of Ford buildings of the twenties," Hildebrand stresses the high degree of integration between manufacturing processes, equipment and other factors, and the physical structure." Hildeband, *Designing for Industry*, 100–101, 108.

[69] Kidder, *Willow Run*, 46–47.

[70] Sorensen, *My Forty Years with Ford*, 281–82.

[71] Cohen argues that the structure's "L" shape and strategic location on the Wayne–Washentaw county line, also responded to Ford's antiunionization efforts. See Cohen, *Architecture in Uniform*, 94.

[72] Kahn, "Don't Let War Plants Scare You," 27.

[73] Hyde, "Assembly-Line Architecture," 14. This solution suggests analogies with the emergence of the setback skyscraper incidental to the legislation of a "zoning envelope." Paul Louis Bentel, "Modernism and Professionalism in American Architecture, 1919–1933" (PhD diss., MIT, 1993), 301.

[74] Kidder, *Willow Run*, 113–14.

[75] Ibid., 121–22.

[76] Ibid., 51.

[77] Ibid., 52.

[78] Ibid., 71.

[79] Ibid., 92.

[80] Cohen, *Architecture in Uniform*, 124.

[81] Ibid.

[82] Didier Fassin and Mariella Pandoflfi, *Contemporary States of Emergency: The Politics of Military and Humanitarian Interventions* (New York: Zone Books, 2010), 15.

[83] Harootunian, "Remembering the Historical Present," 471, 478.

[84] Federico Bucci, "From America to Europe: Stories of Temporary Architecture," *Exporre* 10 (1991): n.p.

[85] Ibid.

[86] Kahn, "Don't Let War Plants Scare You," 28.

[87] Bucci, "From America to Europe."

[88] Abramson, "Obsolesence," 110.

[89] Cohen, *Architecture in Uniform,* 124.

[90] Hyde, "Assembly-Line Architecture," 7; Gleick, *The Information,* 171.

[91] Meister, "Albert Kahn's Partners in Industrial Architecture," 90, 93. The Kahn brothers' capitalization on its reinforced-concrete system is a striking illustration of the "new ways in which [architects] involve[d] themselves in the construction industry" after World War I, described by Paul Bentel. Bentel, "Modernism and Professionalism in American Architecture," 20.

[92] Cohen, *Architecture in Uniform,* 322.

[93] Lefebvre, *The Production of Space,* 42.

[94] RACER, "RACER Trust Open House Wednesday at Willow Run Features U.S. Government's Jay Williams, Mathy Stanislaus," 2013, http://racertrust.org/News/9705.

[95] Ben Austen, "Post-Post Apocalyptic Detroit," *New York Times Magazine,* July 11, 2014, http://www.nytimes.com/2014/07/13/magazine/the-post-post-apocalyptic-detroit.html?_r=0.

[96] Camilo José Vergara, "American Acropolis," *New Statesman,* January 12, 1996, 16–19.

[97] See Amy Elliot Bragg, "Brick + Beam Selected as a Knight Cities Challenge Finalist," *Preservation Detroit,* 2015, http://preservationdetroit.org/2015/01/13/brick-beam-detroit-selected-as-a-knight-cities-challenge-finalist/.

[98] Lee Rodney, "Art and the Post-Urban Condition," in *Cartographies of Place,* ed. Michael Darroch and Janine Marshessault (Montréal: McGill–Queens University Press, forthcoming).

Focus on the 2014 Fitch Colloquium

1. Michèle Pierre-Louis presenting at the annual Fitch Colloquium at Columbia University Graduate School of Architecture, Planning, and Preservation. Courtesy of Hatnim Lee.

Resourcefulness

Michèle Pierre-Louis, former prime minister of Haiti and executive director of the Knowledge and Freedom Foundation, focused on Haiti's heritage preservation, which is paralyzed in the face of the country's increasingly severe challenges: galloping demography, degraded environment, economic and political quagmires. She argues that, paradoxically, this may be the moment when specific experiences in Haiti involving underprivileged populations will give rise to a new understanding of their own environment, of their own capacity to affect their history in the making, and consequently to see themselves as agents in the preservation of their heritage. A sense of resourcefulness can constitute the basis for a thought-provoking dialogue of universal scope about the value of preservation.

FUTURE ANTERIOR: You have held an incredibly diverse range of positions in your career. Could you start with explaining your background and how you came to be involved in preservation?

MICHÈLE PIERRE-LOUIS: I was born and raised in Haiti, but I studied abroad in Paris first, and then in the United States. While I was studying I never thought of spending my life in foreign countries. It was very important for me to return to Haiti after graduation, even though we were still under the Duvalier dictatorship. I was only eighteen years old when I left Haiti and had a sense that I knew very little about my country. When I went back, I worked in a wide variety of places because it was important for me to get an understanding of the general landscape in Haiti. I had studied economics, so I started working in the private sector, then for the government, then for the NGOs, then for myself creating my own enterprise, and then consulting on many different projects. These experiences gave me a better understanding of my country: its history, its political system, its social makeup. It was during this time that I became very passionate about history, and perhaps that is what led me to preservation. I toured the country, visited the provinces and far remote rural areas, discovered unbelievable treasures, and became worried about losing the treasures of the past.

Future Anterior
Volume XII, Number 2
Winter 2015

2. This house was bought by Fondation Connaissance et Liberté (ΓOKAL) and turned into a school for craftsmen while being restored. Courtesy of FOKAL.

For a long time and on several occasions, I was called on to work in the government. I always refused, because I thought it was much more useful to work with civil society organizations. In 1995, I met George Soros; he had become interested in Haiti and wanted to open and finance a foundation there. I was hired as executive director, and our foundation (Fondation Connaissance et Liberté [FOKAL]; www.fokal.org) was created in June 1995. In 2008, I was chosen by the president to become prime minister, and I assumed these functions until November 2009.

I have always been interested in history and in historical artifacts. However, after the earthquake of January 12, 2010, I was called to coordinate a restoration project whose purpose was to save a very important architectural heritage, the "gingerbread houses."

FA: How did you come to think of preservation and politics together?

MPL: It all depends on the meaning you give to politics. Politics for me goes back to the Greek understanding of the common good and the public interest. If we agree on this meaning, preservation cannot be remote from politics. Preservation *is* an element of politics inasmuch as it is a part of our past and our identity, complex notions that we have to deal with. And in that sense, to me, civic engagement toward preservation should be a permanent objective if we are to have a sense of our culture, our identity, our history, nationally and worldwide.

FA: What role then, would you say that the local community in Haiti played in your work? How do you engage with the local community?

MPL: The question is important: how do we engage a community so that the people have an understanding of what heritage and preservation mean, and most of all how can they get involved? In some cases, as we have experienced in a project undertaken by our foundation, creating a public park in an impoverished neighborhood, it is important to maintain a level of constant community dialogue to explain, to discuss and debate, and also to obtain feedback and reactions. This is not necessarily a guarantee of success because there are so many other factors at play, but there will be no success if the community is not involved. It is a major challenge but depending on the pedagogical approach that you develop and the trust that is built among the different stakeholders, progress can be measured.

FA: What role do you see for international organizations in local preservation work?

MPL: This is the other side of community involvement, the support you can get from international expertise. And at this stage, it is not just a question on funding. Of course, financing preservation projects is important, but technical assistance is sometimes even more crucial. In our gingerbread house restoration project, our foundation was able to acquire a gingerbread house that was badly damaged by the earthquake. We turned this house into a craftsmen school thanks to the collaboration of two international partners, the World Monuments Fund, which is in New York, and the Wallon Institute for Preservation, in Belgium. WMF provided much-needed expertise by sending a team of highly recognized preservation architects and the Belgian institute sent us the experts in technical knowhow: master masons, master carpenters, specialists in termites, etc. The collaboration has been and still is absolutely productive and we could not have achieved what we have done so far without their understanding of our goal and their generous and intelligent collaboration.

FA: How did your organization deal with the loss of traditional craftsmanship?

MPL: To create the craftsmen school, we selected twelve young men who had just graduated from four Haitian professional schools. We invited them to be interns in the restoration project we were launching with our partners in the gingerbread house we had bought. They were going to learn by doing, in situ. They did. Under the instruction of our international team who traveled several times a year to teach these young

3. Artisans in FOKAL's training program restoring one of the gingerbread houses. Courtesy of FOKAL.

4. Artisans in FOKAL's training program restoring one of the gingerbread houses. Courtesy of FOKAL.

men renovation and preservation techniques and also what heritage, *national* heritage in that case, is all about. They became so engrossed in the process that now they can explain to every visitor the importance of restoration and how proud they are to have benefited from such a rare experience. I must say that they have done a remarkable job!

FA: Education is of course an investment in the future. Where do you see Haiti in fifty years?

MPL: I dream of a capital city, Port-au-Prince, renovated or rebuilt with parks, monuments, sites, with inclusive neighborhoods, with gingerbread houses and other historical heritage that are a constant reminder of what Haitians can achieve, with libraries equipped with modern technology for the children to learn about history, about the Caribbean, about the world. Haiti has a lot to show to the world! Yes, one can dream! When we come back to reality, I also know that there are so

many challenges facing us: demographics, economy, climate change . . . But it's important to have a vision of the future.

FA: The Iron Market restoration received a great deal of attention in the international media. Could you talk about its reception in Haiti? Do you think that it revitalized the city?

MPL: The Iron Market is a very important monument that was built in the nineteenth century. It embellished the city and was very useful for commercial exchanges of goods and crafts. For lack of care, it became degraded, caught on fire, and at the time of the earthquake there was practically nothing left. So the reconstruction project was well accepted by the government and all those who were able to collaborate. But perhaps the process of rebuilding should have considered more community involvement and a more pedagogical approach to the meaning of the historical monument. Nonetheless, the project's architect was able to gather a whole lot of artisans who worked on the new Iron Market and that is also important.

FA: Could one read your project for a new public park as an extension of your preservation work and of your efforts to protect the public good?

MPL: Yes. In addition to the gingerbread house restoration project, I also coordinate an even larger project: the creation of a public park. In 2007, my colleagues and myself were able to convince the government of Haiti to save about eighteen hectares (approximately forty-five acres) of private wooded properties in Martissant, a neighborhood in the outskirts of Port-au-Prince, fifteen minutes from the National Palace. The GoH accepted and declared the properties (the owners had died) state property. The condition was that our foundation (FOKAL) agreed to sign a contract with the government to create and manage the park. We did. Today, seven years later, it is a beautiful place visited by more than fifty-thousand people last year and composed of several features: a memorial to the victims of the earthquake, which is a wonderful garden; a cultural center with a library in the name of Katherine Dunham, an African American anthropologist who visited Haiti in the 1930s and became so interested by the culture that she bought a piece of property in Martissant in 1954, which is today part of the park; and a medicinal plant garden, as we have the mandate to create a small botanical garden.

There are more projects in the pipeline, and we hope that by the time our contract with the government expires in 2020, we will have achieved all our plans for the park and most of all designed and put in place the governing body that can ensure continuity and sustainability of what is considered today as a model. One major achievement is, as I said earlier, community involvement so that the neighborhood inhabitants have a sense of pride and ownership, an innovative transformative process that also gives hope and dignity.

1. Adam Lowe presenting at the annual Fitch Colloquium at Columbia University Graduate School of Architecture, Planning, and Preservation. Courtesy of Hatnim Lee.

Datareality

Adam Lowe is the founder of *Factum Arte,* a multidisciplinary workshop exploring the union of digital and
physical artistry, and its application to what he describes
as "noncontact" conservation and preservation. *Factum
Arte* is unique in that it seeks to bridge the divide between
traditional craft conservation skills and new technologies
of documentation by producing exacting facsimiles of
heritage objects. Based in Madrid, he has worked on preservation projects with many world-renowned institutions,
including the National Gallery, the Museo del Prado, the
Louvre, The Vatican Museums, and the Fondazione Giorgio
Cini. *Factum Arte*'s internationally acclaimed preservation
projects include the facsimile of Veronese's *Wedding at
Cana* in San Giorgio Maggiore in Venice and the facsimile
of the burial chamber of the Egyptian Pharaoh Tutankhamen, which was recently installed at the entrance of the
Valley of the Kings next to Howard Carter's house. Heritage, he argues, can no longer be thought of in terms of
unique immutable objects. Digital technology has thrown
heritage into a new reality where scanning and printing,
dematerialization and rematerialization, blur the boundary
between the physical and the virtual, the tangible and the
intangible. The digital is no longer linked only to the virtual
and now has a physical presence. According to Lowe, we
are witnessing the rise of a new "datareality" that is related but not the same as materiality, and that will change
how we think and practice preservation.

FUTURE ANTERIOR: *Factum Arte* sits at the intersection of technology and craft, and you are continuously stressing the union of
these two fields. Do you envision craft always playing a part in
the practice of conservation, or is there a time when craft will
be completely obsolete?

ADAM LOWE: Contact conservation is a craft, and the final appearance of the conserved work is evidence of the transformations that have been enacted on the surface. In an ideal world,
all conservation would be completely objective — completely
verifiably objective, but of course that's absolutely impossible.

Future Anterior
Volume XII, Number 2
Winter 2015

So what you see, which is a very important part of *Future Anterior*'s interest, is attention paid to the biography or career of an object. When you're looking at a painting like Veronese's *Wedding at Cana,* you're primarily seeing its history from the end of the eighteenth century to the present day. It was cut into sections and ripped off the wall and taken to Paris, and then put back together and repainted, because there was quite heavy paint loss. There was then a series of conservation attempts that went on in the Louvre that changed the painting in significant ways. That's a relatively straightforward biography. There are many other paintings that have moved from one place to another. Recently, I was in Dresden and looking at the collection there. It was fascinating, because I'm much less familiar with German restoration styles. You can start to see different approaches to different paintings in different places, and you can watch how their career changes or alters depending on where they've been, how they've been valued, what qualities have been prioritized, and what have been suppressed. I think one of the roles that technology has to play is in helping us unravel and understand better the career of each of these objects. And as we understand the way they've changed, we also can see the people who've changed them, so you see the different values in different places at different times being projected upon one ideal form. There will always be a need for building bridges between technical skills and manual skills in the way we document. It's a myth to believe that anything is documented objectively. Different photographers would light the same sculpture in different ways, and that would be a different style. *Factum Arte* has its own procedures which constitute a style as well, one that is completely different from other people. And yes, it's subtle, but there are different styles. In all restoration, the current generation of conservators is critical of the actions of the previous generation. That in and of itself demonstrates the subjectivity of the treatment. As new methods come along and are adopted, they become flavor of the month until someone else raises issue with what's being done. Paraloid was the great savior of restoration and now it's seldom used, or at least frowned upon in most museums.

FA: Where do you see subjectivity arising in your work with *Factum Arte*?

AL: Well there's subjectivity on every level, but we try to understand it and minimize it. For example, even in the design and building of the laser scanner, and the writing of the software, there's a great amount of character, rather than subjectivity. Subjectivity is always put in opposition to some notion of objectivity, but I prefer to think of all the instruments we

2. *Factum Arte*'s facsimile of Veronese's *Wedding at Cana*, in the refectory of the San Giorgio Maggiore, Venice. Courtesy of *Factum Arte*.

use as having their character, and the character is very much the result of the dominant designer. In the case of our Lucida scanner, it's the character of Manuel Franquelo, who conceived it, and has built an absolutely beautiful scanning system that has extraordinary advantages, and has solved many problems in terms of the documentation of surface of objects. I think there is objectivity and character at every level, and obviously the person who writes the algorithms controls the way some things are formed. The way the designer identifies and resolves "issues" determines its character. How we merge and stitch the data introduces another level of character. It's basically a series of mediations, and what you need to do is to understand the transformations that happen at any mediation. Then you can see both the subjectivity and where the objectivity might lie.

FA: Can you highlight a certain example where that character in building the machine really dramatically affected the end product of *Factum Arte*'s work?

AL: Yes. So for example, most scanning systems are effectively abstracting their data as they go along. They're turning a world out there with a surface into a cloud of points in three-dimensional space. The Lucida scanner does that, but it also captures the data as a grayscale image file. Rather than abstracting the object, the Lucida condenses it. So in the future, when there's more computational power, or more ability to process the data at higher resolutions, we'll be able to treat that grayscale data very differently from the way a point cloud can be treated today. Other than interpolating between the points, which is giving you an average, the grayscale data will actually be able to be processed at higher resolutions in the future. That's a very good example of the character of the scanner. Another example is in how the scanner works, by finding a mathematical center to a laser line using a number of mathematical programs and computations. We've been able to refocus the laser so it's finer and can find its mathematical center more accurately. We've also put a lot of work into understanding how speckled noise (a physical phenomenon that exists in the space between the eyes of the cameras and the surface of the object) can be understood to give us better and more pure data from very diverse surfaces.

FA: So you talked a little bit about precision in your presentation. Could you elaborate on how you determine your level of precision, or what's the threshold for your documentation of objects?

AL: 3D scanning, like 3D printing in a way, is a relatively new topic. We're constantly trying to clarify exactly which bits of data, statements, or which commercial assertions are true, and which aren't. I fully understand that anyone designing a scanner wants to communicate to the biggest audience, but very often the machine can't perform according to its specifications. Our interest is in scanners that can deliver data that has a close correspondence to the surface that's being recorded.

I think that's a slightly different approach from many technologically driven or metrologically driven systems. I wouldn't ever claim that our Lucida scanner is the greatest measuring device — it isn't! If I was trying to measure from one point to another, it probably couldn't perform this as well as many other devices or point-measuring systems. But what I would claim, from all the evidence, is that the data recorded with the Lucida of the surface of paintings has a much closer correspondence than any other data set I have seen — there is more information and less noise. There maybe systems that perform specific tasks better, but taken as a whole, the Lucida works!

FA: Do you see these tools as eventually being universalized and distributed or accessible to people with less technological backgrounds?

AL: Yes, this is important. The Lucida scanner is very easy to use. It's been designed to be that. Because really what we want is an operator in Egypt with a relatively good knowledge of computer skills and a reasonable knowledge of photography to be able to learn to operate it very quickly, and to be able to do high-level troubleshooting. Again, one of the reasons we moved away from high-resolution point clouds to tonal data is that we can handle the data with normal image-viewing software rather than expensive 3D software. So certainly I would hope that in ten years' time all the major museums are scanning the surfaces of their artwork before restoration. The National Gallery in London is leading the way. Apart from anything else, the most important thing that we're trying to do is provide the data to monitor the condition of objects. Recent events in Iraq with Islamic State's iconoclasm prove how important this is. Documentation is essential and facsimiles will have an important role to play—in the case of Tutankhamen's Tomb, or in the case of Veronese, there are applications for the rematerialization of the data. But much more important than that are the archives where you can bring together many different types of data in the same place, facilitating a new study and understanding of the object.

FA: Do you think that the spread of these innovative technologies will draw people from outside of the field, bringing more interest to preservation itself?

AL: Yes, I think that's happening. For example, with our facsimile of Tutankhamen's Tomb, people are looking at an object that makes them wonder, "Wow, how did they do that?" To me, it's staggeringly important that people who know their history, who know their painting, who know their spaces and architecture, can have an emotional and visceral response to a work they know is a copy. This certainly suggests that there's a lot of work that needs to be done on understanding the relationship between a copy and an original artwork—work that needs to be done by auction houses and tourists alike.

FA: You mentioned in your talk that, when you work, you would like to be able to replicate the experience of all five senses. Could you speak a little bit more about this?

AL: That's what we're working on. Old facsimiles of paintings were either painted by hand, which are inherently subjective in lots of ways, or they have a false-textured surface. In the '70s, there was an attempt to print paintings on canvas, and to add in impasto paste. But that looks very false, and it looks wrong. But if you can really merge surface, color, tone, and density,

3. Interior of *Factum Arte*'s exact facsimile of Tutankhamen's burial chamber, Valley of the Kings, Egypt. Courtesy of *Factum Arte*.

you can get somewhere toward making an object that, from a normal viewing distance, looks like the original object. Our interest is really in going further than that. If you can go into a facsimile of the tomb and it smells the same, the acoustics are the same, the touch is the same, and the temperature is the same, you can start playing with the synesthetic nature of our response to digital information, where the experience becomes completely multisensory. One of the projects we completed last year was for the Hereford Cathedral, in which we scanned the surface of the Mappa Mundi, which was painted on a single large cow skin in about 1300. The vellum over time reveals its history—it has holes, scratches, and undulations, and has been repaired numerous times. We managed to make a landscape out of the surface of the map, where each of the letters that are painted in black or gold is actually in slight relief. By exaggerating the relief, we were able to make a landscape surface that the blind can touch. But also, it enables you to see the map in a very fresh way, because when the surface is made physical and separated from the color, it makes you think about many different things, but particularly the relationship between the vellum itself and what's drawn on it.

FA: The work you've done on tombs in Egypt raised questions about cultural imperialism couched in terms of Western professionals determining how non-Western countries should care for their cultural objects. What agency or right do Westerners have to record or reproduce such works?

AL: It's very important to understand that our work has absolutely nothing to do with cultural imperialism. We're working for the Supreme Council of Antiquity, who are the Egyptian owners, and have worked under three different governments. We're making a transfer of all the skills and the technologies, so that the majority of the work may be carried out by local Egyptian operators. Our project is therefore generating employment, providing new skills, and transferring the responsibility for the protection of the Theban Necropolis to the people whose lives depend on it. In a way, the Theban Acropolis is located in Egypt but is of supreme importance to the world. The most important heritage sites transcend national boundaries, so the preservation of cultural heritage should, in an ideal world, not be limited by the national boundaries within which it falls. So many of the countries with some of the greatest heritage have limited means to protect them from mass tourism, or from war and conflict. My sense is that the world needs to work together. So in this case it's absolutely nonimperialist. What we're trying to do is aid the people whose responsibility it is to protect and document the object, to create a time-slice documentation of the object. In 2007 that's what the Veronese looked like. In 2009 that's exactly what the surface of Tutankhamen's tomb was. And for me that data is critical to monitor it. But it's also desperately important that the custodian, in this case the Supreme Council, is the person that benefits if any money is to be made from that data. Either from current uses or from future applications.

One of the issues at the moment is that technology is changing so fast that we often don't know how the money will be derived from it in the future. It's desperately important that cultural institutions, whether it's the Louvre or the National Gallery or the Supreme Council, retain all the copyright to the data that's been recorded, and that we use the money derived from it to ensure that documentation and conservation can be carried out on other sites and other works of art. There are ways of generating significant revenue from cultural heritage for the purpose of its own preservation, especially with a growing tourist world. But it's desperately important that money stays in the loop and doesn't just get taken out by governments and applied to different things.

FA: In other words, when you do a project, you're not focused solely on the recording and storing of data, but you're also seeking to leave the skills that you used behind.

AL: Right, so in Egypt, by the time we leave, they will have a group of fully trained scanner operators, being able to work with laser scanners. They'll have photographic operators being able to carry out composite photography. Our interest is, without a doubt, to leave trained teams able to document objects. But equally, it's to build the facsimile workshops. Also, I think the response we've had leads me to believe that the visitors are really ready, and they want to become part of a force that's willing to protect these sites, rather than to think about themselves as a destructive force. And I think what we're finding is there's a real shift in attitude, rather like what I think happened with the "green" movement, where there's a real awareness that unless we change our attitudes, humanity can be a profoundly destructive force. And in exactly the same way mass tourism is putting a kind of pressure on our heritage objects, whether it's the Sistine Chapel or the National Gallery in London or the Louvre, nothing can take that many visitors. You can arrest it, you can create some degree of stability in the short term, but the number of people needs to decrease while it is projected to grow. That's the core of the problem.

A few years ago, in 2012, the BBC published a short piece about what we were doing in the Valley of the Kings. A couple of Australian tourists were saying "we'd never travel here to see a fake," but two years later, you get a real awareness, with people saying, "I never knew we were doing that much damage." So that's the first part: actually getting people to understand why a dynamic environment in a tomb is problematic for its long-term survival. When the tombs are sealed and the temperature stays constant and the humidity stays constant, there's no movement of air and everything's static, the tomb will remain for a long time. But the minute you have the temperature and humidity fluctuating, and dust, you get an environment where something's breaking down.

FA: So you see your work almost as protective of the original artifact in some ways?

AL: I think the whole motivation for what we're doing is to ensure that, whatever happens to the original artifact, there is the data of how it looked at a specific moment in time. We've got a very beautiful project at the moment with the National Gallery in London, where we're recording a painting by Bellini before the restoration starts, during the restoration, and at the end of the restoration, so that you'll be able to compare the changes to the surface of the paint and to the surface of the panel at different times during the restoration. And you'll be able to compare how it looked before the restoration began and after the restoration finished. Very much I see the work we're doing going absolutely hand-in-hand with the work being carried out by traditional conservation and restoration departments.

4. Exterior of *Factum Arte*'s exact replica of Tutankhamen's burial chamber, Valley of the Kings, Egypt. Courtesy of *Factum Arte*.

These two things are not in opposition. It's not either hands-off restoring or hands-on restoring, it's about using all the tools at our disposal to actually understand the things we're trying to care for better. But we have to be aware that in other parts of the world, from Bamiyan to Nimrud, the articulate objects are the battleground.

FA: Where do you see the practice of historic preservation going in the next fifty years?

AL: I think the use of technology to generate forensically accurate evidence will lead the way on almost every front. I hope that a new school of digital restoration will become part of every physical restoration process. If we can try out certain hypotheses on the high-resolution data, and start to have discussions about the aesthetics of conservation, then I think we'll be in very exciting territory.

1. John Ochsendorf presenting at the annual Fitch Colloquium at Columbia University Graduate School of Architecture, Planning, and Preservation. Courtesy of Hatnim Lee.

Structure

John Ochsendorf is professor in the Department of Architecture at MIT and founding partner of Ochsendorf DeJong & Block. His research on historic masonry structures and other alternative structural systems has brought renewed interest in historic preservation as a source of inspiration for contemporary design. Our contemporary engineers, he argues, are primarily familiar with the two materials of steel and reinforced concrete, and are therefore inadequately trained to make decisions regarding historic structures. Remarkable historic structures were demolished or altered because engineers didn't fully understand them. Achieving a fuller comprehension, argues Ochsendorf, demands a deep engagement with both the technical and the cultural aspects of the built environment. Ochsendorf offers three points as a model for engineers working in preservation today. First, "be humble: the builders knew at least as much as we know, and they probably knew more." Second, "assume that the structure is safe, then try to prove it." Third, it is important to "work in an interdisciplinary team to debate a range of solutions." Too often, the word of one structural engineer is taken as gospel, and the result is unnecessary, detrimental change to an ancient building. Engineering can be the greatest threat as well as the clearest opportunity for sound stewardship of cultural heritage, and Ochsendorf's more comprehensive approach shows a promising path for the decades ahead.

FUTURE ANTERIOR: How do you think your background as an engineer, historian, and educator has influenced your definition or view of preservation?

JOHN OCHSENDORF: Maybe a small clarification to begin with—as an undergraduate, I studied at Cornell in structural engineering and also archaeology, so I had a background in both of those fields. I looked very seriously at graduate school in archaeology or preservation in applying my engineering skills. I came to the conclusion that those fields needed engineers, and so I decided to continue my education in engineering. But while I was at Cornell, I took two really significant, for me, graduate

Future Anterior
Volume XII, Number 2
Winter 2015

2. 3D-printed model of the Pantheon dome, used by the MIT Masonry Research Group to perform collapse simulations. Courtesy of MIT Masonry Research Group.

courses in preservation from Michael Tomlin. So that gave me both a sympathetic view of the field and also an appreciation of its expertise. But I would say that our work really crosses boundaries between engineering, history, and preservation. And the truth is that preservation is such a broad umbrella that it reaches into many different fields, and unfortunately, the depth that it reaches in engineering is not as deep as it should be. There's incredible depth in preservation engineering, if you think about the world of conservation and understanding the chemistry and treatment of materials of all kind, yet we don't have the same level of depth in my own field of structural engineering. So that's really my life's work and my life's passion, to bring greater depth to the engineering of traditional materials.

FA: What was it about preservation that first drew you in or got you really excited about the field?

JO: In my engineering education, I was really unhappy about the fact that the questions were all so tightly constrained, they only had one answer, and I was missing the broader, cultural implications of technology. So when I came to study archaeology, it was everything I'd been looking for in the tremendous breadth and the real link to the human culture and to our past. Preservation is a natural joining of those two fields, because if you asked yourself where archaeology meets engineering, you might say it's in the preservation of old structures, for example, or of human culture broadly. I did explore seriously the idea of taking a more traditional path into preservation. From my own experience in studying Incan suspension bridges in Peru, I had learned that what allowed me to make a contribution to archaeology was that I had the engineering training, and that if I could continue to deepen my engineering training, then I could offer even more to the fields of preservation and archaeology.

FA: Your exhibition "Palaces for the People" was extremely popular and well received by the public and press, particularly here in New York. What were some of the challenges of designing an exhibition about the Guastavino vaulting?

JO: It was a project that had its roots almost fifteen years ago, when I was lucky enough to work in Spain, and became exposed to Guastavino vaulting while collaborating on an exhibition in Spain. We worked very diligently over the past eight years to create the exhibition and bring it to the public. We were adamant that a story as rich and powerful as the Guastavino family's could not be told from any one discipline, so we assembled a truly multidisciplinary team of architectural historians, immigrant historians, archivists, architects, and myself representing engineering, and tried to ask, "How do we bring this story to the public?" The thing that was most exciting about it was that we really were successful in bringing it to the broader public. I think the name Guastavino is quite well known in preservation circles, particularly in the northeastern United States and in New York, but it's astonishing how little known the story is more broadly. We had about 100,000 people see the exhibition in the three cities. That was hugely fulfilling and I think we have an imperative to bring the story of preservation and the story of the built environment to the public. It's not an easy thing to do, but it's a necessary thing to do if we're going to strengthen and raise awareness for the value of our field.

FA: Part of the success of the exhibit was that you had several different visual components to the exhibit. You had the images, the photos, the drawings, and then you had the amazing mini vault. Was that part of seeking a stronger engagement with the public?

JO: I have to give credit to the NEH, the National Endowment for the Humanities, because they were the primary sponsor for the exhibit, and they demand a broad engagement with a lot of audiences. They were constantly forcing us to think hard about how we were going to engage young audiences, special audiences, and the general public, too. That meant having a combination of strategies, including multimedia approaches. I'd like to talk about the case of the model for a moment, because this was a full-scale vault replica, and it really represented my values of technology applied to preservation. We had students design and build it in collaboration with masons, so at the same time that we were building the vault for the exhibition, we were really recovering some knowledge about how these vaults were built. That collaboration took place over the course of several years, with masons and with students working side by side to recreate a Guastavino vault. But it was more than just a vault; it was really an anatomical dissection of a vault, because we left it open in the center, so we took away the mystery about what this is. That was probably the single most fulfilling aspect of the entire exhibition for me—seeing students of engineering and architecture working side by side with masons. Let me just say that the students learned much more from the masons than the masons learned from the students. I think that speaks to how the exhibition tried to tackle this story on many different levels, but we can't forget that our field is tangible and physical, and that the trades have largely been neglected in the professional conversation. I would like to see a much greater strengthening of the trades in preservation, and I think that's a much wider symptom of our culture in architecture and engineering and where we are in the United States today, in that the trades are not closely linked with this professional world. We saw this exhibition as an opportunity to bring these two worlds closer together.

FA: Much of your research has focused on safety of historic monuments, and the design of sustainable infrastructure. How do you think preservation and sustainability overlap? In your view, where do they overlap?

JO: They overlap hugely. I think sustainability and the broader goals of sustainability are related to the so-called "Triple Bottom Line"—economics, environment, and society. I would say that it's also related simply to good design, and good preservation is good design. I'd like us to get to the point where the life-cycle valuing of the economic value of cultural heritage, as well as the inherent environmental benefits, are addressed in how we normally operate. We're not there yet, but clearly preservation has a lot to offer the world in terms of trying to reduce our footprint on a finite planet, and I think preservation needs to really strengthen its arguments in this area. The statement that "The Greenest Building is the one that's already been built" is true in many cases, but we need to be more quantitative about it, because sometimes there are bad buildings. Sometimes bad buildings shouldn't stay up. Not every building deserves to be maintained for centuries. Part of that calculation about cultural heritage also has to include a calculation about environmental

3. Guastavino brickwork in Grand Central Station's historic Oyster Bar. Courtesy of Michael Freeman.

and economic worth. We're doing some studies now in various places around the world, really trying to quantify from an energy standpoint, as well as from a quality of life standpoint, whether it makes sense to renovate or renew, and it's not always clear.

FA: What would you say particularly about mid-century, early glass buildings, like curtain wall structures? There's been a lot of talk about how unsustainable they are, particularly because they have a lot of cold joints. The Yale Art Gallery is a great example of a wonderful retrofit. Do you think that this will be an increasingly important problem that engineers will need to address?

JO: I think that is one of our greatest challenges, and in particular we are losing a lot of our twentieth-century heritage. The preservation of that heritage requires new ways of thinking about engineering. But a big part of that is looking at the energy performance of those buildings, as well as the materials of those buildings. There was a tremendous amount of experimentation in the twentieth century, and we learned from it. But there were also a lot of failed experiments. To what extent are we obligated to maintain failed experiments for centuries? I think that's where we have to make very careful judgments about what we value. And I think what you picked up on is exactly one of the key tensions, and it's something that we'll be grappling with in the decades to come.

FA: You continue to stress the importance of the development of the field of preservation engineering. How does it differ from the contemporary professions of conservation and design, and what challenges does preservation engineering face that are different from its related disciplines?

JO: If you ask the question in the United States, "What is a preservation engineer, and how do you become one?" I would say it's largely through practice. We have a lot of engineers who are working in preservation, and who are incredibly knowledgeable from being out, in, and among buildings. But what's also missing is the theoretical underpinning behind how you analyze, for example, a dome made of brick. If you study structural engineering in the United States and almost anywhere in the world, you're taught that there are primarily two materials: steel and reinforced concrete. And the actions of those two materials are very different from traditional materials like a brick vault or a dome. So an engineer armed with a master's degree or even a PhD in steel or reinforced concrete is actually very ill-prepared to analyze and evaluate a two-hundred-year-old brick vault. And so when I say that preservation engineering as a field needs to develop, I mean across the board. We need a greater emphasis on the curriculum, on the fact that much of the work of engineers today deals with existing buildings. Just imagine that, with an engineering education, you can go through six years of school and be taught only theory surrounding new construction, and then you can go out to work for a company, and day after day your work involves dealing with existing buildings. There's a mismatch there. Several decades ago, our curriculum matched when our cities were rapidly expanding and our population was rapidly expanding, but the truth is that we are not preparing engineers well to deal with the realities that they face upon graduation. We need to strengthen this area of preservation engineering from the undergraduate programs in the universities all the way to practice. One thing they're experimenting with in England and in a few different countries is the notion of a certificate program for engineers, where you receive a license as a preservation engineer who's certified to work in cultural heritage, because you've gone through a certain amount of training and exposure to traditional methods of construction and appropriate calculation methods for traditional buildings. There's a lot of work to do, but change doesn't come easily, as the faculty in universities are not typically engaged in these problems. Because preservation engineering is not nano-, bio-, or info-, it's perceived as being an area of low research funding, or of low national importance. Yet that couldn't be further from the truth. Preservation is a subject of international importance, not just environmental and economic but also cultural.

FA: Would you say that England or other countries in Europe are more developed in preservation engineering, or they have a model that's closer to what you'd like to see in America?

JO: I think wherever you go in the world there are examples of exemplary practice and there are examples of substandard practice. I think some countries have a little more of an enlightened approach about the engineering of traditional materials, and I do put England in that category. In the twentieth century, they put a lot of reinforced concrete into Gothic cathedrals, and they recognize now that it was not a good idea. There are many countries in the world that haven't yet recognized that Gothic cathedrals do not desire a reinforced concrete interior.

FA: How do you feel that preservationists and engineers should interact with countries outside of Europe? You've done a lot of work with grass suspension bridges in South America. How should we as Western professionals approach indigenous culture?

JO: We have to be very wary of cultural imperialism, and my strategy as an engineer, which perhaps comes from a background in archaeology and anthropology, is that I don't enter into a new location or a new topic without a guide. I regularly work side by side with art historians, archaeologists, and anthropologists. In the case of Peru, my entrée into the topic and culture there was through working with a Harvard-trained anthropologist who had been living there for two decades, and who spoke Quechua. I could really get a lens into the culture as well as into the unanswered research problems through him. For me, it's absolutely imperative that we as engineers come in with new methods, because too often engineers have an answer for what is the wrong question. I think that to be successful in our research and practice, we have to come up with the right questions, and to come up with the right questions, you really need to be guided by others. One of our principles is that we work in a very multidisciplinary way, with historians and architects. Another principle is that we never propose just one solution. We debate a range of solutions. Although this runs counter to engineering education, when you're dealing with an existing building, there's never just one answer. The same is true in design, but when you're dealing with an existing building, I think thoughtful engineers and preservationists can offer up a spectrum of solutions, and then those solutions can be debated from the Triple Bottom Line. I think that if we are really to be successful as a discipline, what we have to be bringing to the world of preservation is a spectrum of ideas. Too often what I see is engineers offering a single solution. Of course that gets to the question of the value of engineering, and who's willing to pay for the time to come up with multiple solutions. But I think this is what our cultural heritage demands. As an example, can you imagine if a leading work of art, for example one of the great paintings of the world like the *Mona Lisa,* were labeled endangered by an engineer or conservationist, who insisted that it must be dipped in epoxy immediately, to preserve it for future generations? What if this were carried out without a peer review, or without a spectrum of solutions offered? What is happening right now with the great monuments throughout the world is that, too often, the word of a single engineer is resulting in a predetermined intervention without a critical review. That for me is tragic, when a building has survived in some cases for millennia, and then the word of one individual can drastically alter it. That's literally where we are today as a profession. And it isn't only the other engineers who are complicit, because the surrounding community is often complicit, because if you work with a single engineer who presents you with one solution, and then you accept that, then you're also

4. Guastavino staircase at Carnegie Mellon University, Pittsburgh, Pennsylvania. Courtesy of Michael Freeman.

complicit in the work's alteration. We need to demand more from engineering.

FA: You seem to be saying that the complicity of the interdisciplinary community of preservationists, architects, and heritage consultants stems additionally from a lack of engineering knowledge. Therefore, the word of the engineer is automatically taken as the gospel.

JO: Sure, and what are you going to do if you're the client? If an engineer comes and they have a Master's degree from an important university and they say, "This is what has to be done." The client complies and says, "Okay, the engineer has spoken."

FA: How do you think preservation should or will change in the next fifty years?

JO: I personally would like to see a strengthening of the role of engineering as a responsible player in preservation. But I also think the field of preservation must advance the sophistication of arguments related to life cycle performance of the built environment in every aspect—culturally, from a quality of life standpoint, as well as from an environmental and economic standpoint. Additionally, I think that a deeper theoretical underpinning for preservation is important, because the field has grown tremendously. We're well beyond, say, a microscopic treatment of horsehair plaster, which is important in one specific project, but the growth of a deeper theoretical underpinning as exemplified by *Future Anterior* is really important. And yet, what I would like to see to make us more relevant, not only to criticism and theory but also to national leaders and to the future of human society is a strengthening of the arguments regarding the different disciplines, and in those different areas. Otherwise, preservation is not central to the human endeavor, and I think it should be. You feel that when you walk down a successful traditional street almost anywhere in the world—you feel that value. So how do we harness that, and how do we leverage that power to convince policymakers that preservation is the best thing we can do for society?

1. Ilaria Cavaggioni presenting at the annual Fitch Colloquium at Columbia University Graduate School of Architecture, Planning, and Preservation. Courtesy of Hatnim Lee.

Flexibility

Ilaria Cavaggioni is director and coordinator for architecture for the Superintendence for the Architectural and Landscape Heritage of Venice and Lagoon. Cultural tourism, she argues, has fundamentally changed many historic cities into tourist lodging and entertainment complexes addressed exclusively to the tourism market. Such newer and faster dynamics of transformation cannot be adequately solved by traditional preservation expertise. The answer to these pressures, Cavaggioni asserts, is flexibility. We need to imagine architecture according to new principles of flexibility to respond to this new reality without sacrificing preservation ideals of artistic quality and historical continuity. She urges preservationists to change our view of historic buildings from static things to elements of a broader developmental process. "It is no longer possible to think that historical buildings are untouchable," she argues. This does not mean, however, that every space is an appropriate candidate for adaptive reuse; context and discretion must constantly be considered and balanced, with interventions that "show the building's identity . . . but without being necessarily and uselessly shocking." To follow the principle of flexibility requires searching for an architectural language capable of expressing past, present, and future as a continuity, so that contemporary work does not stand in the way of our relationship to the past or become an obstacle for tomorrow.

FUTURE ANTERIOR: How did you become involved in preservation?

ILARIA CAVAGGIONI: I would say that my interest for preservation, long before becoming a professional choice, was a real youth passion. When I was at school I had already started studying and practicing the specific techniques for stone and fresco preservation. But later I realized I wanted to study architecture, because I thought it was more interesting to be part of the process and to work in the specific area where the theoretical principles are transformed into ideas and then into actions on the buildings. Although I studied architecture and completed the necessary exams to become an architect, the ultimate goal

Future Anterior
Volume XII, Number 2
Winter 2015

for me was to work on the preservation side, and my studies were thus focused. When I finished, I was quite lucky because I started working on an important project, the restoration of one of Palladio's villas; it was the same villa that I had studied for my thesis project, so it was an amazing experience to follow the project from its initial stages into the completion of the work. That experience has been, I think, fundamental for my future and for my approach to built heritage, because it helped me understand how important it is to be close to the reality of the building, and to study everything in detail — all the traces, all the constructive details that can help to understand part of the transformation processes that occurred during the centuries — because the building can tell you many, many things about its past. In fact, I have used this cultural approach in nearly all of the later projects that I have engaged in.

FA: For those unfamiliar with Italian preservation, could you describe the Soprintendenza?

IC: My office, the Soprintendenza, is the local office of the Ministry for the protection of cultural heritage and landscape: so we have the central ministry at the national level and then local superintendency at the regional level. We work on the side of the state, using public monies for the repair and conservation of buildings that belong to the state, but we also control all of the private works for nationally listed buildings. We try to experiment and test techniques and carry out research so that we can improve the work that we do and address the private works with specific guidelines.

FA: What are some of the challenges that you have encountered working in Venice?

IC: I would say that Venice is, of course, a unique city because of the way that it was built and the way that the buildings are realized; the fact that it is surrounded by water is an uncommon situation, but the main aspect of its particularity is its continuity with the past, which is one of the biggest challenges that we deal with. Many feel that Venice is a city where nothing has changed, but this is not true: things have changed over the centuries, but these modifications are slow and are very much in continuity with the past. There has never been a breaking with the past, and that is probably why modern architecture has not found much space in Vènice, because Modernism seeks to break with the past, to make something completely different, to not relate to the past. In Venice, this continuity in the changes is fundamental. It probably comes from the fact

2. The Arsenale in Venice is a complex of former shipyards and armories clustered together. Courtesy of Ilaria Cavaggioni.

that there is a very high continuity in the use of the materials and techniques: buildings in Venice, both in the past and in more recent time, have been mostly realized with the same and simple materials such as wood and bricks and lime. The constructive techniques have changed very little.

This idea of continuity also relates to the fact that historical buildings have to address climatic changes and the fact that the soils are sinking. This is why, probably, the techniques and materials have remained the same over the centuries and for this reason today, preservationists want to recover traditional techniques and skills and the artisans and culture that we have partly lost over the last century. We need to recover it if we really want to preserve the cultural heritage of the historic cities and particularly of Venice.

FA: There is also modern architecture in Venice, such as the projects by Carlo Scarpa or Tadao Ando's Punta della Dogana. Would you approach the preservation of these modern buildings any differently?

IC: Well, we have already worked for the preservation of some of Carlo Scarpa's projects, like the Foundation Querini Stampalia, which has been recently repaired. We have quite a deep knowledge of how to preserve old buildings but we have little experience with modern or contemporary architecture. So I think that the cultural approach for repairing modern architecture comes from our experience with old buildings. We follow similar principles when dealing with newer buildings, because it is still important not to lose the materiality of these constructions and to save as much as possible.

But while we accept that historic buildings are the result of transformation processes over the course of centuries—that they are not homogeneous, that they have been transformed, that they may be not completed—this is more difficult to accept for modern architecture. In modern architecture, I think, the form, the geometry, the details, the use of new materials, is very important in order to define the architectural project. We accept, for instance, that historical buildings are not completed and that they have missing pieces, but it is hard to accept modern architecture in this way. If we think of the huge cube of concrete that was realized by Tadao Ando inside the Punta della Dogana, that is a pure form, a pure solid, a pure volume; you cannot accept it if it is not perfectly conserved. Could you imagine if the Villa Savoye had been stabilized in its ruined state? This can be acceptable for premodern historical buildings, but not for modern architecture. We feel we need to recover the original form of the architectural elements even if that means replacing them, something we wouldn't do with historical buildings. Part of this is also because modern architecture was realized with the same materials that are still used today, so it's quite easy to replace and reproduce the steel and concrete that Carlo Scarpa used in his construction, much easier than to replace old bricks or plaster.

FA: You seem to suggest that it is important to think of historic buildings as always incomplete, while simultaneously striving for their completeness.

IC: In preservation you often have to engage with paradoxical situations: if we want to reuse historical buildings we need to repair them but, at the same time, we want to make every effort to preserve the building and its materiality, because we know that the physical traces that you recognize on the surfaces of the building are part of its history. The other day, I was on the scaffolding to control an example of new plaster realized in order to reproduce the historical surface. Looking very carefully we found small fragments of the first finishes of the surface, which was a very thin coat of plaster made with lime and stone dust with the signs of the joints that were pressed there. You can just have fragments, but those fragments are so important because they help to give you an idea of what the building originally looked like. We have to make every effort to preserve all of this if we don't want to lose the identity of the heritage, but at the same time we have to work in details to identify the spaces that are appropriate to receive the modernity without compromising the integrity of the old space.

3. The large central court of the Punta della Dogana Contemporary Art Center in Venice, Italy, by Tadao Ando. Courtesy of Ilaria Cavaggioni.

FA: What role do you think sustainability might play in the future for preservation and conservation, particularly in Venice, where climate change is going to continue to be a major issue?

IC: I think that conservation and sustainability have more or less the same goals. Traditional architecture, historic architecture, was very sustainable; when Palladio designed his buildings, for example, he thought about where it was necessary to put the windows to respond to architectural principles, but also to produce a passive ventilation in the building. Traditional building techniques were often also very sustainable. In Venice, for instance, there is a very typical kind of building construction, the so-called *battuto* floor, which is a very thick flooring constructed of crushed brick, broadly used in Venice because it can move but doesn't break or crack, it flexes with the building. This technique was made reusing the terracotta tiles, and so the process itself was very sustainable. Moreover, I think that in recovering, in repairing and preserving historical buildings, in some way, we are already working sustainably.

FA: What role can preservation play in the equation between sustainability and tourism?

IC: Venice has a very serious problem with cruise ships that cannot be resolved just by thinking about the ships. It is

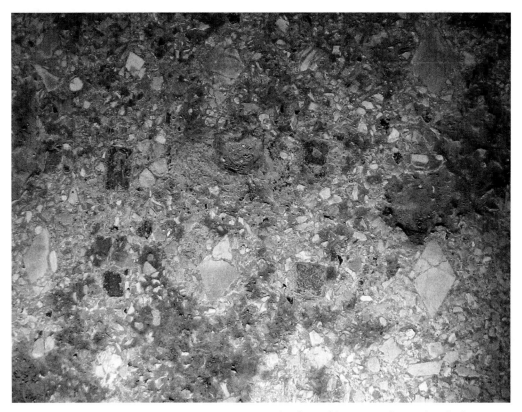

4. Battuto, or flooring made of reused
materials, typical in Venice.

necessary to question how ships can arrive to the city by sea,
ensuring completely safe conditions both for the historical
buildings and for the environmental context of the lagoon. The
location of the harbor for the city and all related decisions are
political ones with serious consequences. Today the tourism in
Venice is unsustainable, but we have to create different goals
and interests for this sector and solicit different ways of living in
the city. Many people who arrive on cruise ships don't understand that they are entering a sea city where people, using the
traditional boats, have lived on water for centuries; the cruise
ships let people admire the city from a particular and high view-
point but they don't make you feel like you are crossing the fragile context of the lagoon. The risk is to have an iconic vision of
the city but miss its real meaning. In fact, there are hundreds of
traditional, small boats that cross the canals, and people should
be more involved in this endeavor, in learning how to use these
boats, how they work, how they worked historically, and how
they are built: this would help tourists to be closer to the real life
of the city and would address them to different interests.

FA: Do you think climate change will continue to be a major
issue for preservationists in the future?

IC: I don't think that climate change will have a huge influence
in the future, because I think that technology today is prov-

5. The new interior volume of Ando's insertion weaves around the existing structure. Courtesy of Ilaria Cavaggioni.

ing that it is able to face these environmental problems. The challenge for preservation, I think, will be in maintaining its relevancy; the care of buildings cannot be an end unto itself— we have to produce more cultural experiences for people. Cultural experiences in historic buildings give the opportunity to people to see their own experience in different ways and at different levels, generating new ideas. It's a way to widen our knowledge and the culture of preservation involving the existing buildings. For instance, up to ten years ago, the Biennale strictly took place inside the buildings of the Arsenale or inside the Giardini. But in the past ten years, there have been many collateral events, and the organizers have worked very hard to make these events part of this exhibition by locating them inside historical buildings. As a result, we now have hundreds of private buildings that are opened to the public during the Biennale, and people can visit them, which you couldn't do before. These buildings have been repaired and preserved and have been incorporated into a dynamic process so that we are now able to have a much larger city that people can visit. This is a way to expand our cultural value, giving people the opportunity of making different cultural experiences.

1. Tim McClimon presenting at the annual Fitch Colloquium at Columbia University Graduate School of Architecture, Planning, and Preservation. Courtesy of Hatnim Lee.

Community

Timothy J. McClimon, president of the American Express Foundation and vice president for Corporate Social Responsibility, American Express, recognizes the importance of the communities that surround issues of heritage. As the leader of the company's endeavors in the field of historic preservation and community engagement, McClimon aims to increase the exposure of the work of preservationists to their community members, toward a much larger goal: the longevity and survival of our historic places. While funding the efforts of preservationists and conservationists worldwide, McClimon argues that the root of financially securing the future of a significant object lies in its integration to the community. Public engagement, awareness, and activism on behalf of historic sites pave the way for the development of future donors. The idea of service to a community, a core value of AXP and the American Express Foundation, is one that McClimon believes to be a powerful tool for framing and strengthening the work of the preservationist today and in the foreseeable future. AXP has been engaging communities in historic preservation since 1995, when the organization started collaborating with the World Monuments Fund on the now-famous Watch List. In 2006, the National Trust and AXP began the Partners in Preservation program in San Francisco, later moving on to successful campaigns in Chicago, New Orleans, Boston, Minneapolis, Seattle, New York, and Washington, D.C. By the time the program concluded seven years later in Washington, D.C., it had awarded 15 million dollars in grants, engaged over 1.5 million participants, and helped 82 percent of the historic sites increase visitors, with an average growth of 310 percent. Today, in the age of social networking, communities form and understand themselves differently than in the past. McClimon stresses that preservation must adapt to the new importance of social media and digital outlets to efficiently present information at a faster pace to a wider audience. Preservation's role in today's social interactions is no longer an isolated strand of interest but rather a part of vast networks of aims, goals, and interests that compose the contemporary community.

Future Anterior
Volume XII, Number 2
Winter 2015

FUTURE ANTERIOR: How is American Express approaching the relationship between sustainability and preservation?

TIM McCLIMON: While we haven't funded many specific projects, I think there's a strong relationship there, and it's something that the National Trust for HP has been studying themselves. The National Trust has a green center—it's located in Seattle— that is focused on public policy and helping communities develop policies that would help preserve historic sites as environmentally friendly sites. That's great, but I would like to take it a step further to supporting some of the sites them- selves and think about them as entities that have an impact on the environment. What could we do to lessen that impact?

FA: What is next for your work in preservation now that the Part- ners in Preservation (PIP) project is over?

TM: The National Treasures program is an evolution of PIP. I think that we started out thinking that the reason the National Treasures program would be attractive and impactful is that instead of focusing on just one community in a year—which is how we approached PIP—this would take the whole year of preparation: of selecting the sites, training the sites and social media, advertising, having the voting period, and then grants.

FA: It's a lot of preparation.

TM: It was a year-long program for every city, which was great individually, but we weren't doing anything in the rest of the country that year. The National Treasures program gave us and the National Trust the opportunity to focus on communities that might have one historic site, or one project, which needed help. Be it a campaign associated to save it, or preserve it, or what have you—which wasn't necessarily tied to just one place per year. I think that is a great concept and a great idea, and I think that the way that it's been executed has been fine. We have funded some projects—like the Miami Marine Stadium in Miami. It is a terrific project, and we've helped orchestrate planning and feasibility studies for the restoration of the 1965 modern concrete stadium, and we've helped restore the ceiling at Union Station in Washington as well. Those are two National Treasures projects, and we have a couple more that we're going to announce soon. What is it that we can do with that program to make it more engaging in communities? That's something I think we need to figure out.

FA: How do you go about trying to identify the next steps for the program?

TM: You just get ideas from people. A person I just met downstairs was from Houston and had a terrific idea. She said, why don't you make the "National Treasures" the "National Treasures Communities." Then, focus on communities that have more than one site, like historic areas, or communities that have a number of different interests, which brings us back to a scope similar to Partners in Preservation. But I can see where if you just expand the idea beyond the individual site—which is where the National Treasures focus is right now—just expand that a little bit into the community around the site, the neighborhood around the site; what is it that we can do to make that community more sustainable? As a way of protecting that place. Maybe there's something there. But this is an iterative process. And somebody will have an idea, just like an *American Idol* idea fed the beginning of Partners in Preservation.

FA: You mentioned that one of the things that helps these projects to be successful is the notion of "keeping it local." But it also sounds like there's a proper boundary around what qualifies as local. What's the community boundary, how do you find it? How do you negotiate that between projects?

TM: Well, for some projects like Partners in Preservation, it was readily identifiable as a metropolitan area. But for projects that are outside of that particular program, I think it depends on the community. You have to take that on a case-by-case basis. It's one of the great things about coming to meetings like this: people come up to you and they give you ideas. Another individual I met downstairs works for the park service on the Erie Canal, which is going to celebrate its centennial in 2016. The Erie Canal is five hundred miles long. What's the community there? Is it just the businesses along the canal? Is it everyone along the canal? Is it the park itself? I think it's going to change

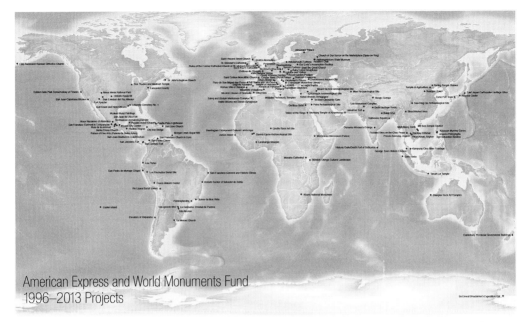

American Express and World Monuments Fund
1996–2013 Projects

3. American Express funded several international World Monuments Fund sites. Courtesy the World Monuments Fund.

from place to place. We just funded a project at the Grand Canyon. The community at the Grand Canyon is going to be different than Erie; we funded another project over at the Park Avenue Armory on the Upper East Side of Manhattan. What's the community of the Park Avenue Armory? It's probably not the neighborhood around it. In fact, some members of the community around the Armory dislike the armory because it attracts so many people. So it's the people that utilize the Armory as a place for arts events and cultural events — it's the people that come from all over to that site that are the community there. Like the Grand Canyon, it's the people that come there, the tourists. One of the projects we did with a sustainable tourism program is to create a visitors center at the Galapagos Islands, for example. The Galapagos Islands — people would just go. The tour group says go, and there was no tourist center; there were no tour guides ever that were sanctioned by the park service. So we helped create a sustainable visitors center there, which has really cut down on these sort of rogue visitors.

FA: You mentioned in an interview with *Forbes* in 2012 the notion of a networked society and that no one institution can do its work in isolation anymore. What do you mean by that?

TM: In a networked society — a sort of ecosystem if you will — no one entity, be it a government or corporation or wealthy individual or the public, can do everything. So we do need all of these people partnering together, which is why we called it Partners in Preservation to begin with. The program was all about partnerships and getting people to work together, including the community that may be either living around the

4. American Express's commitment to public-minded monuments dates back to the nineteenth century, when the company helped raise funds to build the Statue of Liberty pedestal. Courtesy the American Express Corporate Archives.

site or working around the site or going to the site and not even realizing that it's a historic place, or not even realizing that it needs restoration or that it needs money, or that they can become a member of an organization. So I think you all have to do what you can and play the role that you have the expertise and the resources to play. We play that role more from a marketing standpoint because we have marketing expertise as a company, and we also play it from a resource standpoint because we have resources—but we don't have the expertise to make the selections of the sites. That's not our thing.

1. *1 x Unknown (2012–)* (Quiberville), production still. Photograph by Margherita Moscardini. Courtesy Ex Elettrofonica, Rome.

How to Preserve a Bunker
1 x Unknown (2012–)
Margherita Moscardini

The Atlantic Wall along the coast of Europe and Norway is in ruins. One of Hitler's military infrastructure projects, known as *Führer Directive No 40,* transformed natural coastal lines into Fortress Europe. There are about fifteen hundred such Nazi bunkers. Now they lie mostly in ruins, too costly to preserve or to demolish.[1] Some of the concrete bunkers have become unmoored from their foundations and are rolling onto the beaches below, slowly migrating, as if they were giant boulders, dissolving back into minerals. Since Paul Virilio's pioneering *Bunker Archeology* (1975), they have become the object of countless studies and photographic surveys. *1 x Unknown (2012–),* an ongoing artistic research project by Premio New York–winner Margherita Moscardini, offers new and unusual light on the subject. First exhibited at MACRO Museum in Rome in 2012, the project seeks to rethink *Bunker Archaeology* and to explore the history and continued relevance of the European shorelines as reconfigured during World War II. Moscardini has since exhibited aspects of this project in Rome's Ex-Elettrofonica Gallery in 2013 and 2014.

Art and Silence
For three years Moscardini interviewed bunker residents, tracing their extreme and exotic lives as they transformed bunkers into private pavilions, exhibition spaces, external kitchens, and disco bars.[2] The bunkers became a backdrop for an anthropological investigation of alterations, omissions, broken narratives, and the imperfections of human memory. *1 x Unknown* presents the buildings as if they were by-products, shadows, of these human narratives. Although collected and classified, traditional historical documentation was partially concealed so that the final work is purposefully not comprehensive. It is composed of fragments of mixed media: photos, architectural plans, drawings, and documentary videos, next to which Moscardini presents vials with sands and masonry fragments collected on site. Perhaps following the trope of twentieth-century art history that absence is stronger than presence, her more traditional historical research was hidden, or never fully revealed, neither in the exhibition layout nor in the project catalogs.[3] The work, one surmises, is purposefully decontextualized within the space of the museum or gallery.[4] The question is why. This intentional semi-silence and quasi-invisibility

Future Anterior
Volume XII, Number 2
Winter 2015

fig. c

fig. d

2. *1 x Unknown (2012–)* (partial view and view of the installation). Ambient size, n.7 mini-projectors, power packs, prints, paper, paperboard, concrete, n.7 miniDV videos, MDF. Photograph by Dario Lasagni. Courtesy Ex Elettrofonica, Rome.

can be interpreted as one manifestation of the "unknown" in the work's title, a powerful metaphor of the passing of time, of sand being turned into concrete then released back into nature, of dust to dust. One could also read the willing concealment of the historical research as an attempt to express the fact that the bunkers are in many ways manifestations of military secrecy. They were the direct result of top-secret orders and global military ambitions of the Third Reich. *1 x Unknown* returns them their enigmatic status.[5]

The unavoidable difficulty comes in squaring off this willful concealment of research with the fact that *1 x Unknown* is cast as a research project. Moscardini's research focuses primarily on bunkers in abandoned areas or sites under the threat of demolition. She collects maps; architectural plans and sections; and information about political, social, geographical, and geological realities. This research is then translated not into a book but rather into artworks. Her process of translation is rather protracted, with a preparatory process followed by an incredibly long-term, presumably infinite project. She reads the ruin as a medium and scans its "geo-morphological background." She also documents the tastes, dialects, and behaviors of local communities.[6] Each of the bunkers, for Mascardini, is a work of sculpture, an object and a model of itself at 1:1 scale. She examines these ruined objects as texts, coded with layers of meaning that are often unrelated or irreconcilable, such as Virilio's theory of military technology, and the many civilian lives lived in the bunkers. She is interested in the gaps between these overdetermined readings of the bunkers. Her work has us consider how the sheer materiality of the bunkers cannot be fully captured by such interpretations. Her vials

fig. b

3. *1 x Unknown (2012–)* (details). Ambient size, n.7 mini-projectors, power packs, prints, paper, paperboard, concrete, n.7 miniDV videos, MDF. Photograph by Margherita Moscardini. Courtesy Ex Elettrofonica, Rome.

of decontextualized, ruined materials cue us to the manner in which meanings can give way to silences, perhaps secrets, or even yet-to-be-written philosophies.[7]

Minerals and Memories

1 x Unknown is also a chemical experiment of sorts, but one unlike any traditional materials in conservation laboratory work. An important ingredient of the installation is a sequence of handmade cement folders for digital screens that contain research information on Moscardini's personal Bunker Archeology, placed on plywood platforms as testing grounds or laboratory tables. Produced synthetically from chemical formulas, crystals, and powders of various grey shades found on site, these newly mixed materials encourage us to consider their previous incarnation as bunkers. This attention to the materiality of concrete, to its aggregation and disaggregation over time, creates a particular fiction about the material. Moscardini writes:

> the process of erosion seems to have completed the original design of the fortifications: intended to blend into their surroundings. Modeled by intersection of wind and tides, they have ended up resembling the raw material extracted and then used in their construction: sand, dug up in situ to be transformed into the concrete.[8]

Here Moscardini taps into a long tradition of architectural theory that has defined concrete as an imitative material. Adolf Loos claimed that if "'every material possesses its own language of forms, and none may lay claim for itself to the

4. *1 x Unknown (2012–)* (details).
Ambient size, n.7 mini-projectors,
power packs, prints, paper,
paperboard, concrete, n.7 miniDV
videos, MDF. Photograph by Margherita
Moscardini. Courtesy Ex Elettrofonica,
Rome.

forms of another material,' then concrete, an indiscriminate
borrower from the forms of every other material, turned out to
be without a language of its own."[9] More recently, Jean Louis
Cohen explained that concrete presents as a series of theoretical dichotomies. It is, for example, both solid and liquid: "built
from the very beginning into the assembly of iron rods and concrete, but also into the concrete itself, being a mixture of a solid
substance and water." Cohen continues, arguing that concrete
also stages a "dichotomy between engineers and architects,
generating new forms of professional and business practices."[10]
It lends itself to flights of architectural expression and calcu-
lated restraint of engineering solutions, both of which can be
read into a bunker. But bunkers are not tectonic constructions
in the traditional architectural sense, for, as Moscardini notes,
"every joint would have been a weak point."[11] Instead they are
solid blocks of reinforced concrete made in single pours. They
are closer to decaying monolithic rocks than to architecture.

Forensics

1 x Unknown is forensic. It excavates the Atlantic Wall as the
site of massive crimes and massacres. The bunkers were
commissioned by the Nazi Organisation Todt (OT), which was
named after Fritz Todt (1891–1942), the powerful entrepreneur
and civil engineer responsible for the Thirds Reich's systems
of autobahns, aqueducts, and high-end military advanced
fortifications. After Todt's death in an air crash, the giant architectural and engineering operation became the heart of Albert

5. *1 x Unknown (2012–)* (partial view and view of the installation). Ambient size, n.7 mini-projectors, power packs, prints, paper, paperboard, concrete, n.7 miniDV videos, MDF. Photograph by Dario Lasagni. Courtesy Ex Elettrofonica, Rome.

Speer's architectural empire, still working as a war machine.[12] Like Todt, Speer's early career was in the field of construction, but whereas Todt's special interest lay in the methods of engineering technologies, Speer was focused on architectural planning and the monumentalization and ornamentalization of ideologically and politically charged architecture. However, in terms of his new bureaucratic position, Speer would religiously avoid this discourse on "beauty." Indeed, even under Speer's supervision, Organization Todt would be known not as an architectural studio that produced designs but as a significant part of DAF, or Deutche Arbeits Front (German Labor Front), a war machine operating with overscaled projects, diagrams, and statistics. One of the notorious slogans of Organization Todt gives us a sense of the cold ideology behind the construction of bunkers: "One million labor units, 24/7 working hours, ten hundred thousands tons of concrete powder and sand."[13] Significantly, the bunkers were built without foundations, ignoring one of the basic laws of architecture, in order to satisfy military logic: the lack of foundations allowed the bunkers to be displaced by the impact of an attack without breaking.[14]

The bunker's migratory and unstable location is part of the forensic evidence that Moscardini brings to our attention as part of its historical significance. She balances different media as a way to cross between disciplines—engineering, politics, military–industrial production, statistics, science, forensic science, architecture, law, and poetry—and to evince multiple layers of historical meaning from the bunkers. The meanings invoked could perhaps also be documented in a traditional historical paper but never as compellingly and immediately. Moscardini encourages us to phenomenologically engage with architectural materials, and in doing so she helps us discover

6. *1 x Unknown (2012–)* (stills from video). Ambient size, n.7 mini-projectors, power packs, prints, paper, paperboard, concrete, n.7 miniDV videos, MDF. Courtesy Ex Elettrofonica, Rome.

them in perpetual flux, as evidence of material migration and displacement as a historically charged process.

Reading the Atlantic Wall

"In Quiberville a monolith sat on the beach. It has fallen from the cliff as a consequence of the erosive process. On one hand it can be considered as a big pebble among the others (as a direct part of the context), on the other it is a completely separated object. Three doorways, one next to the other, are on the side opposite the sea. When I get closer I hear the sound of the water reverberating inside: the bunker has become a shell."[15] Moscardini decontextualizes the bunkers, reading them as carcasses of animals (shells) or as mere material (sand used as concrete aggregate, only to decay back into sand). She seems to present the erosion of the concrete as the unintentional fulfillment of the bunker's original purpose and design: to become confused with nature — the bunkers were designed as camouflage. "Modeled by the action of the wind and the tides," states Moscardini, "which act on them in the same way as they do on the surrounding landscape, they have ended up resembling the raw material extracted and then used in their construction: sand, dug up in situ to make the concrete."[16] These concrete monuments both belong to their context and exceed it at the same time.

1 x Unknown is a form of critical preservation through art. It casts light on the historical meanings and importance of the bunkers in a way that no historian or philosopher could. Its complicated, triplicated, multilayered aesthetic structure may allow us to "brush history against the grain"—to use Walter Benjamin's expression—in order to understand the preposterous aspects of our present. Such attentiveness to details might help to explore interstices, disjunctures, and gaps in the present in order to cocreate the future, reminding us that an artistic gesture activates preservation as an instrument for tracing the contours of entangled histories, multiple and conflicting identities, and the migration of narratives and tropes. Moreover, this artistic experiment forces us to rethink and recalibrate the field within the broader trajectory of contemporary visual culture, from the point of view of avant-garde artistic actions, conservation, curatorial practices, law, geography, conservation, and archeology. It may even provide us with a new understanding of World War II bunkers.

Biography
Xenia Vytuleva teaches at the Graduate School of Architecture Planning and Preservation at Columbia University in New York. She has curated a number of exhibitions, including "IMMaterial Box of Innovative Ideas and Materials" (Schusev State Museum of Architecture, Moscow), "Oscillations" (Moscow Exhibition Hall Manege) and "Music on Bones" (MAXXI, Rome).

Notes
[1] John Christopher, *Organisation Todt: From Autobahns to the Atlantic Wall* (London: Amberley, 2014).
[2] Rudi Rolf, *Atlantic Wall Typology* (Stratford, U.K.: PRAK Publishing, 2008).
[3] Margherita Moscardini, *1 x Unknown,* exhibition catalog (Rome: Macro, 2012).
[4] The project *1 x Unknown* has its own intense itinerary, shown in gallery spaces in Rome, Paris, and Seoul. See the interview by Alberto Fiore, "Evoking Space and Architecture," *Arte & critica 72* (October/ December 2012): 69–71.
[5] Materials on the Atlantic wall, including architectural drawings, blueprints, and calculations were among the latest folders of documents to be declassified after the Nuremberg Process. See Christopher, *Building the Third Reich.*
[6] Sara Marini, *Nuove terre: Architetture e paesaggi dello scarto* (Macerata: Quodlibet, 2010).
[7] It was Leon Battista Alberti who first started reading ruins as texts in order to unfold the glory and the meaning of Roman Antiquity. See H. Burns, "Leon Battista a Roma: il recupero della cultura architectonica antica," in *La Roma di Leon Battista Alberti,* 35–38 (Milan: Skira, 1998).
[8] On reinforced concrete breaking the rules of art history, see Adrian Forty, *The Material without a History* in *Liquid Stone: New Architecture in Concrete* (Princeton, N.J.: Princeton Architectural Press, 2006), 22–24.
[9] Ibid., 34.
[10] Jean Louis Cohen, "The Saga of Concrete," in *Liquid Stone: New Architecture in Concrete* (Princeton, N.J.: Princeton Architectural Press, 2006), 22–24.
[11] Moscardini, *1 x Unknown,* 11.
[12] H. Schofield, *Hitler's Atlantic Wall: Should France Preserve It?,* BBC documentary, 2013.
[13] See Christopher, *Building the Third Reich.*
[14] Moscardini, *1 x Unknown.*
[15] Ibid., 9–10 .
[16] Ibid., 10–11.

Anya Sirota

Artist Intervention
Pink on Beige

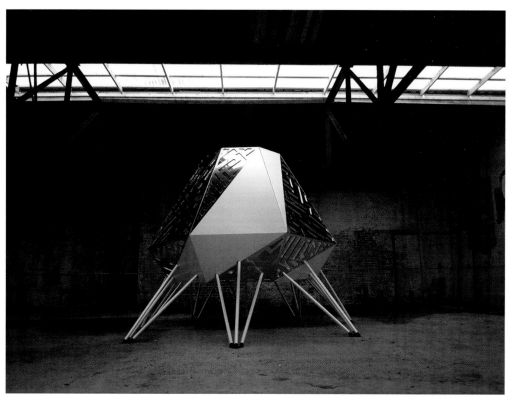

1. *General Manifold,* installation entry, Federal Screw Works, Chelsea, Michigan. In collaboration with Jean Louis Farges and Steven Christensen. Peter Smith, 2012.

2. *General Manifold,* interior view, Federal Screw Works, Chelsea, Michigan. In collaboration with Jean Louis Farges and Steven Christensen. Steven Christensen, 2012.

3. *General Manifold,* installation exterior, Federal Screw Works, Chelsea, Michigan. In collaboration with Jean Louis Farges and Steven Christensen. Steven Christensen, 2012.

4. *Interrobang,* rooftop gallery installation, Packard Automotive Plant, Detroit, Michigan. Jean Louis Farges, 2013.

5. *Interrobang,* rooftop gallery installation, Packard Automotive Plant, Detroit, Michigan. Jean Louis Farges, 2013.

6. *Pop It Up* at Les Tanneries, Amilly, France. Jean Louis Farges, 2013.

7. *Pop It Up* at Les Tanneries, Amilly, France. Jean Louis Farges, 2013.

8. *Pop It Up* terrace wall at Les Tanneries, Amilly, France. Jean Louis Farges, 2013.

Submission Guidelines

Future Anterior is a peer-reviewed (refereed) journal that approaches the field of historic preservation from a position of critical inquiry. A comparatively recent field of professional study, preservation often escapes direct academic challenges of its motives, goals, forms of practice, and results. *Future Anterior* seeks contributions that ask these difficult questions from philosophical, theoretical, and critical perspectives.

Articles should be 4,000 words, with up to seven illustrations. It is the responsibility of the author to secure permissions for image use and pay any reproduction fees. An abstract (200 words), a brief author biography (around 100 words), and a list of numbered image captions with credits must accompany the text. Acceptance or rejection of submissions is at the discretion of the editorial staff. Please do not send original materials, as submissions will not be returned.

Formatting requirements for the manuscript: Text must be formatted in accordance with the *Chicago Manual of Style,* 16th Edition. All articles must be submitted in English, and spelling should follow American convention. All submissions must be submitted electronically, on a CD or disk, accompanied by hard copies of text and images. Text should be saved in Microsoft Word or RTF format.

Formatting requirements for illustrations: Images should be sent as TIFF files with a resolution of at least 300 dpi at an 8 x 9 inch print size. Each image file should be numbered in accordance with the image captions. Figure placement should be indicated clearly in the text, after the paragraph in which they are referenced. Image captions and credits must be included with submissions.

Checklist of documents required for submission:
___ Abstract (200 words)
___ Manuscript (4,000 words)
___ Illustrations (7)
___ Captions for illustrations
___ Illustration copyright information
___ Author biography (100 words)

Please mail all submissions to:
Future Anterior
Historic Preservation Program
Graduate School of Architecture, Planning, and Preservation (GSAPP)
400 Avery Hall
1172 Amsterdam Avenue
Columbia University
New York, NY 10027

Questions about submissions or published articles can be mailed to the above address or to futureanterior@columbia.edu.

Future Anterior
Volume XII, Number 2
Winter 2015

www.arch.columbia.edu/futureanterior

SUBSCRIBE TO FUTURE ANTERIOR

Future Anterior is published twice per year, in summer and winter. Prepayment is required.

PRINT EDITION
Subscription Rates:
• Individuals: $30.00
• Institutions: $65.00
• Outside the U.S.: add $5.00 for each year's subscription.

To subscribe to the print edition of *Future Anterior,* please visit the University of Minnesota Press website at http://www.upress.umn.edu or complete and submit this form with your payment.

DIGITAL EDITION
Institutions may subscribe to the digital edition of *Future Anterior* through JSTOR at http://jstor.org.

PAYMENT | Two convenient ways to pay:

☐ Check enclosed, made payable to University of Minnesota Press. (Checks must be drawn on a U.S. bank in U.S. funds.)

☐ Mastercard / VISA (please circle):

No. _____ Exp. Date _____

Signature _____

ADDRESS | Mail my subscription to:

Name _____

Address _____

_____

Daytime phone _____

E-mail address _____

Mail orders to:
Journals Department
University of Minnesota Press
111 Third Avenue South, Suite 290
Minneapolis, MN 55401–2520

Fax subscription orders to:
612-627-1980

Back issues may be ordered from the University of Minnesota Press website at http://www.upress.umn.edu/.

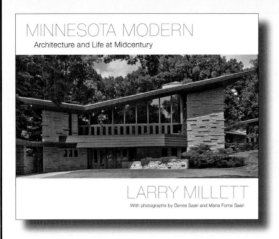
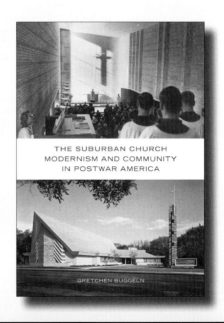

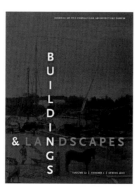

Become a *Future Anterior* Sponsor

Future Anterior is funded by grants and distributed in the spirit of making knowledge available to everyone. Donations are critical to helping us accomplish this mission. If you would like to become a sponsor, please fill out this page and mail it, with a check payable to Columbia University, to:

Future Anterior
Graduate School of Architecture, Planning, and Preservation
400 Avery Hall
1172 Amsterdam Avenue
Columbia University
New York, NY 10027

Or contribute by credit card online at:
https://giving.columbia.edu/giveonline/?schoolstyle=110

All sponsors will be recognized in each issue of *Future Anterior* and receive a one-year subscription to the journal.

Please check the appropriate sponsorship level:

Individual Sponsor: ❑ begins at $100/year
Institutional Sponsor: ❑ begins at $500/year
Patron: ❑ begins at $1000/year

Name*: _____

Address: _____

_____

City: _____

State: _____ Zip: _____

Country: _____

Institution/Office: _____

E-mail:_____
*please provide your name exactly as you would like it to appear in print